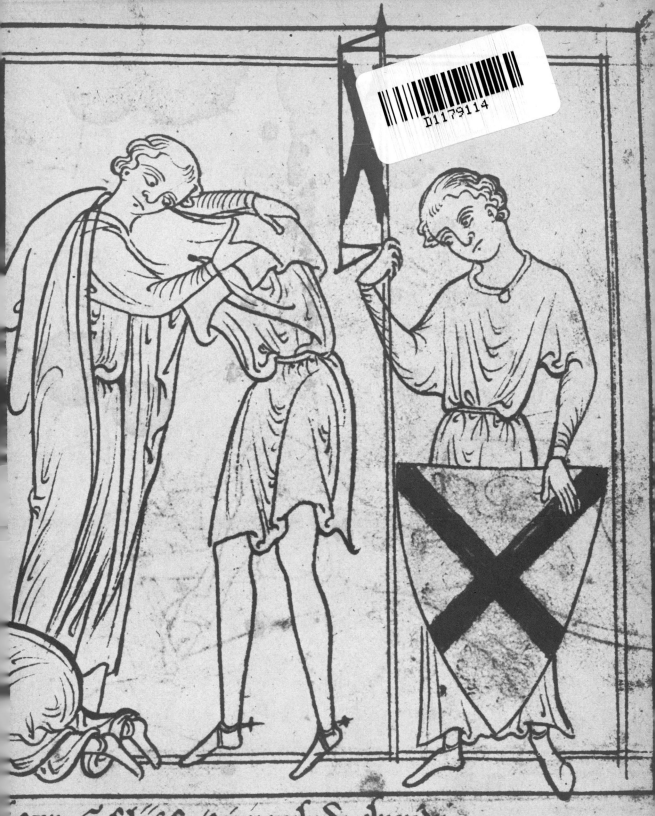

atur cū filiis suis iuuenib; duob; uidẽ
roniby strenuissimus Otta ⁊ milione
idtis̄ aserā cuoq̄ nō minimā mul

The Life and Times of
KING JOHN

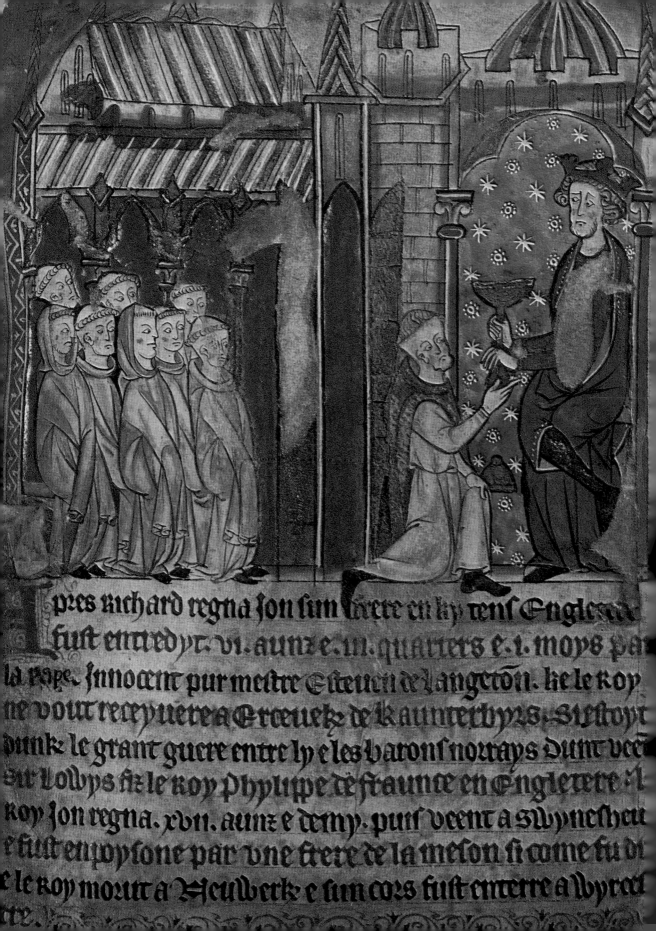

pres Richard regna son fiz frere en ky tens Engleterre
fuit entredyt. vi. aunz e. iii. quarters e. i. moys par
la pape. Innocent pur mettre Esteuen de Langeton. ke le Roy
ne vout receyure a Ercevek de Kaunterbyres. Si estoyt
dunke le graunt guere entre ly e les barons norrays dunt veet
sir Lowys fiz le Roy Phylype de fraunce en Engletere. i.
Roy son regna. xvii. aunz e demy. puis veent a Swyncshou
e fuist enpoysone par une frere de la meson si come su di
e le Roy morut a Neulberk e sun cors fuist enterre a Wyrcc
tre.

The Life and Times of
KING JOHN

Maurice Ashley

Introduction by Antonia Fraser

Book Club Associates, London

Series design by Paul Watkins
Layout by Sasha Rowntree

Filmset by Keyspools Limited, Golborne, Lancashire
Printed in Great Britain by
C. Tinling & Co. Ltd, London and Prescot

Contents

Acknowledgments

Photographs and illustrations were supplied or are reproduced by kind permission of the following. Aerofilms: 108–9, 112–13; Alinari: 164–5; Archives Nationales, Paris: 41; Biblioteca Apostolica, Vatican: 119; Bibliothèque Publique, Dijon: 100; Bodleian Library, Oxford: 3, 19, 51/2, 79, 82, 104, 105, 110 © Professor Boase, 122 © Professor Boase, 176/1, 176/2, 177; British Museum: 2, 15, 23, 53, 54, 76–7, 81, 83/2, 88, 90, 91, 116–17, 129, 142, 144, 147, 150, 151, 153, 154, 160/2, 172, 173/2, 175/1, 176/3, 178, 180, 181/2, 205, 214; British Printing Corporation: 29, 76–7, 89, 95, 96, 97, 98, 104, 105, 152, 160, 161/1, 179; Burgerbibliothek, Berne: 29; Dean and Chapter, Canterbury Cathedral: 35, 83/1; Cathedral Treasury, Aachen: 120; Master and Fellows of Corpus Christi College, Cambridge: 14, 20, 48/2, 49, 101, 121, 136, 146, 156–7, 176/1, 188, 190, 191, 202–3, 207; Courtauld Institute: 31, 35, 167; Department of the Environment: 26–7, 59/1, 169, 184, 194; Durham Cathedral Library: 22; Geoffrey Drury: 36; Giraudon: 41; P. M. Goodchild & Son: 192; Guildhall, King's Lynn: 192; Robert Harding: 171; Wallace Heaton: 170; Michael Holford: 71, 196; A. F. Kersting: 60, 87/2, 138–9, 173/1, 199; Courtesy of the Corporation of London: 170; Mansell Collection: 134; Foto Marburg: 12–13, 16/12; Museo di Roma: 80; National Monuments Record: 80/1, 86/2, 87/1; National Trust: 173/1; Picturepoint: 58; The Pierpont Morgan Library: 47, 50, 62–3, 74, 132, 141; Public Record Office (Crown Copyright): 95, 96, 97, 98, 161/1, 179; Radio Times Hulton Picture Library: 175/2; Jean Roubier: 10–11, 30, 32–3, 44–5, 51/1, 131; Royal Commission on Historical Monuments: 59; Dean and Chapter of Salisbury Cathedral: 167; Scala: 80, 120; Temple Church, London: 36; Thomas Photos: 124; Trinity College, Cambridge: 48/1, 72/1, 72/2, 107, 130, 198, 210; The Board of Trinity College, Dublin: 31; University Library, Cambridge: 38–9, 68–9, 72/3, 92–3; University Library, Heidelburg: 148; Victoria and Albert Museum: 160/1; Dean and Chapter of Westminster Cathedral: 89; Derrick Witty: 189, 200–1; Dean and Chapter of Worcester Cathedral: 189, 200–1.

Numbers in italic indicate colour illustrations.

Picture research by Penny Brown.

Maps drawn by Design Practitioners Limited.

Introduction

THE LEGEND OF Bad King John dies hard in British history. Just as every schoolchild has heard of Magna Carta, that fabled early thirteenth-century foundation of our liberties, the blackened character of the monarch from whom these concessions were wrung by righteous barons is too often the inevitable accompaniment. As a result it has been John's unfortunate fate to develop in our annals as 'an exceptionally maligned King'; and in a particularly fascinating chapter in his biography Maurice Ashley analyses the various stages in this remorseless process. Beginning with the monkish chroniclers who, for their own good reasons, quite early set about his reputation, John then suffered at Shakespeare's hands – his treatment of the cruel death of John's nephew, Arthur of Brittany, leaving a permanent scar on the imagination. It was however in the Civil War period, when the Great Charter became transformed by the opposition to the Crown into the touchstone of freedom, that the prestige of King John suffered its most damaging attack, while at the same time those barons who had contested with him were elevated into latter-day heroes. The great nineteenth-century historians were scarcely kinder, adding moral judgments to the staining of John's character, already defiled by earlier scandals. In short, it was not until our own age that a more balanced appreciation of the truths of medieval history has led to a fairer assessment of this controversial monarch by the standards of his own time.

The youngest of the huge brood of children of King Henry II and his formidable Queen, Eleanor of Aquitaine, John was born in 1167 when his mother was already forty-five – a member of that strange Plantagenet dynasty sometimes called the Devil's brood because they were said to be condemned to fight each other. It was his father, faced with the many territorial claims of his elder brothers, who called him 'John Lackland', and destined him for the Church. But by 1199 the death of Richard I had brought the former 'Lackland' to the throne, to face in his turn the extraordinary pressures of a king ruling in a feudal society. Many of these preoccupations were military –

the problem of raising either a host or the money to hire an army, contrasted with the equal problem of the nobility in peacetime, left to its own turbulent devices. By emphasising the essentially feudal nature of medieval kingship – in John's problems with the Church, for example, it should be remembered that ecclesiastical dignitaries were often at the same time feudal lords – Maurice Ashley enables us to see Magna Carta anew for what it was at the time. Here was no grand 'palladium of English liberties' as it was depicted in the seventeenth century, but on the contrary a feudal compact, in some respects reactionary, hastily drawn up by certain members of the baronage – by no means the whole number – when the demands of his French wars had driven John into the position where he needed to make a few concessions.

Considering the enormously wide powers possessed by the King within the system, if only he could exercise them, John then was certainly no tyrant, any more than his father Henry II or his brother Richard the Lionheart, whose virtues are much extolled in popular romance, had merited the title. John showed himself an industrious, ambitious, hard-pressed medieval monarch, a good administrator, if a bad handler of individuals, hot-tempered perhaps like all the Angevins yet with dreams beyond many of his forbears' of turning Britain into one nation. Long robbed by the subsequent sanctification of Magna Carta of his rightful place in English history, John is here rescued with clarity and sympathy as a complex and in some ways even admirable character, very far from being a mere evil symbol of royal oppression.

Antonia Fraser

Preface

THIS BOOK is not an attempt to whitewash King John. The legend that he was a bad man and a bad king has been destroyed and abandoned by modern experts. In any case it is no longer accepted that rulers can be portrayed as totally depraved or completely saintly. Historians, if they must occupy a judgment seat – and that is difficult to avoid – are capable, like other human beings, of becoming more tolerant as they grow older. At any rate that is how I feel.

I am greatly indebted to Dr Brian Harris for reading this book in typescript and saving me from errors. I am grateful to Professor Frank Barlow and Professor J.C.Holt for help before I started work on it.

MAURICE ASHLEY
February 1972

1 John Lackland 1167-99

QUEEN ELEANOR, the remarkable and beautiful woman who was the wife of King Henry II of England, known as Plantagenet, once told her youngest son, John, that her husband's family, the Angevins, were descended from the Devil. The tradition was that an early Count of Anjou, the House to which King Henry II belonged, had been married to Melusine, who was Satan's daughter, a fact which was discovered because she never attended Mass and when at last she was made to do so, flew out of a high window in the church and disappeared. Thus the Angevins were known as 'the Devil's brood' and brother

PREVIOUS PAGES Effigy of Henry II, the first Plantagenet king, from his tomb at Fontevrault.

was destined to fight against brother and son against father. So indeed it happened in John's lifetime.

Eleanor was a great heiress. As Duchess of Aquitaine she had been the feudal ruler of a rich and vast area of France, including Poitou in the north (of which she was countess) and the wine-bearing district of Gascony in the south-west. Henry was her second husband. She had first been married to King Louis VII of France, a strange and deeply pious member of the House of Capet, who took his handsome and brilliant wife with him on the Second Crusade against the Mohammedans of Palestine,

BELOW Effigy of Eleanor of Aquitaine on her tomb at Fontevrault. As Duchess of Aquitaine she was ruler of almost half of France south of Loire, and her marriage to Henry II brought these lands into the ownership of the English Crown.

13

RIGHT Four kings of
England from the
Chronicle of Matthew
Paris: (above, left to right)
Henry II and Richard I;
(below, left to right)
King John and Henry III.

ABOVE A genealogy of the kings
of England from the Chronicle of
Matthew Paris. Matthew Paris
became historiographer at

St Albans in 1235 and he wrote a
very unfavourable and biased
account of King John
in his history.

during which they lost interest in each other. With some difficulty the Pope induced them to sleep together, but Eleanor could only produce daughters: so the French King had the marriage annulled. Henry Plantagenet stepped in and snapped up the discarded heiress. He was nineteen and she was thirty when they married in 1152. She bore her second husband five sons and three daughters. John, her youngest child, was born on Christmas Eve 1167 when his mother was forty-five. Having done her duty and exhausted her charms so far as Henry was concerned, she first left him for her native Poitou and then was imprisoned for eleven years on the ground that she had conspired with her sons against her husband. Henry II consoled himself with the fair Rosamund Clifford and other mistresses. But Eleanor was to remain a formidable figure long after her second husband was dead.

John's father proved himself to be a successful and acquisitive king who ruled over what has been called the Angevin 'empire' which stretched from the southern borders of Scotland to the north of Spain. He inherited England and Normandy through his mother, known as the Empress Matilda, who was the granddaughter of William the Norman, the conqueror of England. From his father, Geoffrey of Anjou (Matilda's second husband), Henry Plantagenet received the fiefs of Anjou, Maine and Touraine; after the death of his younger brother he obtained control of the duchy of Brittany and the county of Nantes. In the course of time he acquired the border fiefs of the Norman Vexin, Berri and Auvergne. He was also the overlord of Scotland and Toulouse. Thus in terms of concrete power he far outstripped the Capetian kings of France, his feudal overlords, whose own domain covered fewer than 3,000 square miles (about one seventieth of modern France) and was ruled from Paris. Yet when John was born, being Henry II's youngest son, there seemed no prospect of his sharing in this lavish inheritance. At the age of four he appears to have been destined not for the State but for the Church. He was given no fief; and his own father called him 'John Lackland'.

John was born in Oxford, but before he was a year old he was placed under the care of an abbey in Anjou. He can never have had much home life as his father's Court wandered from castle to castle throughout his extensive dominions and his mother

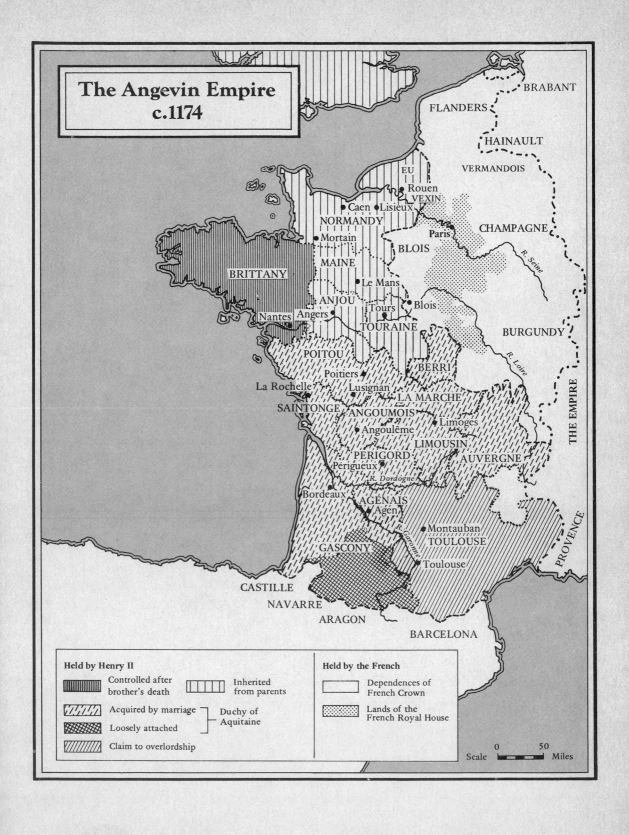

The Angevin Empire c.1174

BRABANT

FLANDERS

HAINAULT

VERMANDOIS

EU

Rouen

VEXIN

Caen • Lisieux

NORMANDY

CHAMPAGNE

Paris

Mortain

BLOIS

MAINE

Le Mans

R. Seine

BRITTANY

ANJOU

Tours • Blois

Nantes • Angers

TOURAINE

BURGUNDY

POITOU

BERRI

Poitiers •

R. Loire

La Rochelle

Lusignan

LA MARCHE

SAINTONGE

ANGOUMOIS

THE EMPIRE

Angoulême

Limoges •

LIMOUSIN

PERIGORD

AUVERGNE

Périgueux •

R. Dordogne

Bordeaux

AGENAIS

Agen

PROVENCE

Montauban •

TOULOUSE

R. Garonne

GASCONY

Toulouse •

CASTILLE

NAVARRE

ARAGON

BARCELONA

Held by Henry II		Held by the French	
Controlled after brother's death	Inherited from parents	Dependences of French Crown	
Acquired by marriage	Duchy of Aquitaine	Lands of the French Royal House	
Loosely attached			
Claim to overlordship			

0   50
Scale   Miles

was soon separated from him. John seems to have mastered the sports of hunting and tournament play at the Court of his eldest surviving brother, Henry, known as the Young King, and his academic education was entrusted to Ranulf de Glanvill, a distinguished lawyer who was his father's Chief Justiciar. An attempt was made to betroth John at the age of five to the daughter of an Italian count, but the girl incontinently died. At the age of nine however he was betrothed to a wealthy heiress, Isabella, daughter of the Earl of Gloucester; she was his second cousin and also, like him, a great-grandchild of King Henry I. They were married, in spite of the Archbishop of Canterbury's indignant protests on account of their kinship, when John was twenty-one, but his bride failed to bear him any children.

Even before his wedding John's prospects had already brightened. It is true that whereas his father had promised the whole of England and Normandy to the Young Henry, Aquitaine to his second son, Richard, and Brittany to his third son, Geoffrey, John had only been offered seven castles in different parts of his brothers' promised dominions. But in 1183 the Young Henry, who had rebelled and thus caused his father much anguish, died. Thereupon John, who had now come to be the apple of his father's eye, was offered the duchy of Aquitaine, while Richard was to take over England and Normandy. But Richard, an energetic and capable prince who was devoted to his mother and to Aquitaine, refused to give it up. John was then invited to become King of Jerusalem, but Henry II wisely turned down this dangerous and dubious proposal even though John begged on his knees to be allowed to accept it. So instead Henry consoled John by appointing him Lord of Ireland.

Ireland was then a poor country divided uneasily between native chieftains and Norman barons. In 1171, with the full approval of the Pope, Henry II had visited Ireland and without fighting subjected it to his rule. Though subsequently the island relapsed into anarchy and many Irish chieftains were assassinated, Henry thought it was a good idea to send his favourite son to Ireland to acquire the arts of warfare and government. Before he left in April 1185 John was knighted by his father at Windsor. But John did not distinguish himself in Ireland. The monastic chronicler, Gerald of Wales, who accompanied the expedition, wrote that John:

An Irishman killing a fellow countryman. Throughout much of this period Ireland was in a state of anarchy as native Irish chieftains and Anglo-Norman settlers warred with one another (Bodleian Roll 187c Fr6).

… being himself young and little more than a boy, followed the counsel of young men whom he took with him, who were utterly unknown in Ireland and themselves knew nothing, whereas he rebuffed the honest and discreet men whom he found there, who knew the customs and habits of the country, treating them as though they were foreigners and of little worth.

John and his young friends were said to have laughed at the shaggy beards of the Irish chieftains. The native Irish defied him and the Anglo-Normans ignored him. After eight months John returned to England, a failure. But the blame was not merely due to the inexperience of an irresponsible prince. The armoured knights whom his father had sent with him were unsuited to guerrilla warfare in wooded country and bogland. English soldiers throughout history have found the Irish hard to subdue.

In 1186 John's brother Geoffrey of Brittany was killed in a tournament but left a posthumous son, named Arthur, to take his title. So once again John was deprived of a profitable

Contemporary illustration of knights fighting in single combat. Trial by combat, in which the accused and the accuser fought each other until one gave in, was a common way of settling quarrels in the Middle Ages. Often those involved did not fight themselves, but hired champions to fight for them.

inheritance. Richard was also disappointed because his father did not bestow upon him fuller power. Thus King Philip II of France (who had succeeded his father, Louis VII, in 1180), a statesman of ability, ambition and cunning, was able to stir up trouble between Henry II and his two remaining sons. The French King launched an attack on the peripheral territories of the Angevin empire in Berri, Auvergne and Touraine. When Henry II, fighting desperately to preserve his inheritance, refused to allow his two remaining sons to go on the Third Crusade (the kingdom of Jerusalem had fallen to the Mohammedans) Philip provoked Richard into attacking his father in Maine and his native Anjou. In the summer of 1189 Henry, worn out and abandoned except by his heroic friend William Marshal, surrendered much territory and money to the victorious French King. All he asked was to know the names of the men who had conspired against him. The first on the list was

20

that of John, his favourite son. On 6 July 1189 the old Plantagenet warrior and statesman died in the church at Chinon in
Touraine, it was said, of a broken heart.

In order to understand the events that followed it is necessary
to recall some of the features of early medieval society in England. Kings did not necessarily succeed to the throne by primo-
geniture: they needed to be related in some way to their
predecessors but they had to gain the approval of their leading
subjects and might win their crowns by conquest and hold them
by military might. Neither Harold II, William I, William II nor
Stephen became king of England simply by hereditary right.
Once a king was crowned, he wielded very wide powers in
theory, but these were restricted in practice. For example, he
had to swear a coronation oath pledging himself to rule according to the established customs of the land, though there might
well be argument over what those customs were. Kings also
had to govern with the aid of their tenants-in-chief, both
secular and ecclesiastic, important men who attended the Great
Councils in the King's Court. If monarchs wished to live peacefully, they had to respect the rights of the Church, which had
been strengthened by William the Conqueror. The clergy had
their own law courts and were not expected to contribute to the
royal treasury except of their own free will. Kings did not govern by divine right; the Pope spoke for the Almighty. So
the Pope could claim to depose wicked rulers and to give
judgment when clergy appealed to him against kings who violated the privileges of the Church. The Pope could also demand
that kings should serve the cause of God. In fact English monarchs were not absolute in the sense that they claimed to be after
the Reformation.

Under the king the social structure was determined by the
use of land in return for services or money payments. In theory
the king owned all the land, which was the principal source of
wealth. He could, besides calling upon his barons or tenants-in-
chiefs for military service, exact reliefs or succession duties,
require aids (payments exacted, for example, for the knighting
of his eldest son or the first marriage of his eldest daughter);
in an emergency he could ask for extraordinary aids; he could
levy fines and enjoy the profits of wardships. In time of war the
free provision of armed knights could be demanded from

tenants-in-chief for a period of two months; in time of peace they might be called up for forty days' service or for the duty of guarding castles. The amount of service was determined by the number of knights enfeoffed by a baron, that is to say the number of knights who accepted the same obligations to their lord in return for the tenancy of their lands as their lord performed for the king in return for his. The king, if he preferred, could compound for knights' services. The barons would then be called upon to pay a 'scutage' (literally shield tax) for every enfeoffed knight on their books. There were in England some three hundred barons and seven thousand knights out of a total population of two million. The scutage was assessed in marks (which were equivalent to two-thirds of the pound sterling) for each knight's fee held by the tenant. The knights and lords of the manor could in turn require services from their tenants, which might be paid in labour or in money or in both. Thus a complicated network of services, rents and customary payments existed; and conflicts of obligation were a main cause of wars, rebellions and social unrest. Greed and ambition prevailed then just as they do now, but the ruling classes could often appeal to feudal custom to do what they wanted to or to avoid doing what they did not want.

What King Richard I wanted when he succeeded his father (he was crowned on 3 September 1189) was to take part in the Third Crusade: this does not seem to have been for religious reasons; in fact he admired the Saracens and once expressed the view that Pope Clement III was Antichrist, but he loved adventure and war. John, on the other hand, wanted to ensure his own succession to his brother's wide dominions if Richard should be killed on the Crusade. Before Richard left England he created his brother Count of Mortain in Normandy, confirmed him as Lord of Ireland, approved of his acquisition of the lordship (or 'honour') of Gloucester gained by his marriage, which took place on 29 August 1189, bestowed on him other fiefs and castles, and assigned to him the entire royal revenues of six English counties, Cornwall, Devon, Somerset, Dorset, Derby and Nottingham. That seemed generous enough; but in fact Richard appointed not John but a Norman upstart, William Longchamp, to take the leading post in the government of England during his absence on the Crusade. Longchamp was

OPPOSITE Crusader knight doing homage. Richard I earned distinction as a Crusading leader, and in 1215 John took the Cross, although it is doubtful whether he ever intended to go on Crusade. BELOW A knight receiving his sword from the King.

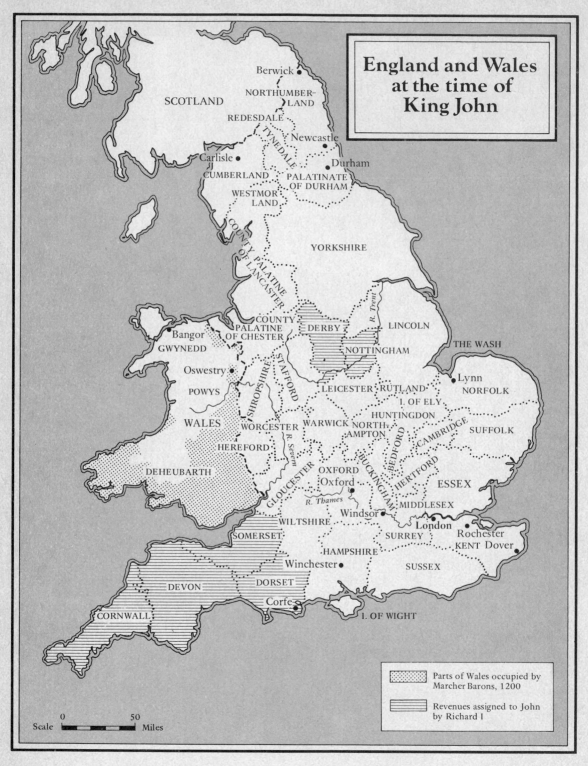

England and Wales at the time of King John

SCOTLAND

Berwick
NORTHUMBER-LAND
REDESDALE
TYNEDALE
Newcastle
Carlisle
Durham
CUMBERLAND
PALATINATE OF DURHAM
WESTMOR LAND

COUNTY PALATINE OF LANCASTER

YORKSHIRE

COUNTY PALATINE OF CHESTER
Bangor
GWYNEDD
Oswestry
POWYS
WALES
DEHEUBARTH

DERBY
NOTTINGHAM
R. Trent
LINCOLN
THE WASH
Lynn
NORFOLK

SHROPSHIRE
STAFFORD
WORCESTER
HEREFORD
R. Severn
LEICESTER
RUTLAND
I. OF ELY
HUNTINGDON
WARWICK
NORTH-AMPTON
BEDFORD
CAMBRIDGE
SUFFOLK

GLOUCESTER
OXFORD
Oxford
R. Thames
BUCKINGHAM
HERTFORD
ESSEX
MIDDLESEX
Windsor
London
Rochester
KENT Dover

WILTSHIRE
SOMERSET
HAMPSHIRE
SURREY
SUSSEX
Winchester

DEVON
DORSET
Corfe
CORNWALL
I. OF WIGHT

Scale 0 ——— 50 Miles

Parts of Wales occupied by Marcher Barons, 1200

Revenues assigned to John by Richard I

24

not only Bishop of Ely but Chancellor and papal legate and later Justiciar, a veritable Pooh Bah. Moreover Richard summoned John to Normandy and ordered him to stay out of England for three years; and as soon as the King reached Sicily on his way to the Holy Land, he sealed the treaty of Messina which named Arthur of Brittany, the four-year-old boy who was his nephew, to succeed him if he should die without issue. Still John must have had high hopes of the succession; after all, the English monarchy was elective; and even were it hereditary, though Richard married for considerations of State, he was a homosexual (like King William II) and was to have no children.

Through the persuasions of his mother, Richard allowed John, after all, to return to England at the end of 1190, and he soon became the focus of resistance to William Longchamp. Longchamp, though able and loyal to his master, was avaricious and autocratic and soon alienated the influential barons and tenants-in-chief. On his return John set up his own Court, refused to allow royal officials into his shires or honours, and played on the grievances of the baronage. It looked as if a civil war might break out between the Justiciar and the King's brother. However Richard heard in Sicily of the unsettled political situation in England. He therefore dispatched to England Walter de Coutances, Archbishop of Rouen, who was in fact a Cornishman, with full powers to do whatever he thought fit. Soon afterwards Richard's and John's half-brother Geoffrey, an illegitimate son of Henry II by the fair Rosamund, also arrived in England to take up his appointment as Archbishop of York (the Archbishop of Canterbury was abroad in attendance on King Richard). Longchamp's agents, who were under the mistaken impression that Geoffrey had come to England without Richard's permission, unwisely dragged Geoffrey from a priory altar and imprisoned him in Dover Castle. Thus Longchamp offended both the lay and ecclesiastical baronage. Walter de Coutances had intended to mediate between Longchamp and Count John. But now he felt unable to do so because Longchamp had become so unpopular.

As it turned out, the arrival of the Archbishop of Rouen did not help John as much as he might have hoped. For it was agreed at an assembly of magnates that Longchamp should be deposed but that Walter de Coutances should act as Chief Justiciar in his

Dover Castle in Kent,
where John's half-brother
Geoffrey was imprisoned
when he arrived in
England to take up
his position as
Archbishop of York.

place. John therefore decided, in order to forward his ambitions, to enter into an alliance with King Philip II of France who had returned from the Third Crusade in 1191. John had good arguments for his behaviour. In the first place, Richard I had set an example by allying with France against his father when he was the King of England. In the second place, Philip was over-lord of the Angevins for all their possessions in France and therefore had an important part to play in the establishment of a successor. Thirdly, should Richard be drowned or killed far from Europe, John was obviously going to be faced with a struggle against the heir his brother had named, the young Arthur of Brittany. But if Philip opted for him, John stood a good chance of acquiring the whole of the Angevin empire. When it was learned in December 1192 that Richard on his way back from the Crusade had in fact been shipwrecked and had fallen a prisoner into the hands of the Emperor of Germany, Henry VI, who held him until the first instalment of a huge ransom was paid, John's hopes soared and he at once hurried over to France to do a deal with Philip II.

Philip II proposed that John should divorce his wife (that would be easy because although John's wife was his second cousin, he had never obtained the consent required from the Pope to marry her), that he should marry Philip's half-sister Alice, and do homage to him for all the dominions which Richard held of the French Crown. John undertook to surrender territory in Normandy and Touraine to Philip in return for his support. An agreement to this effect was sealed in Paris in January 1193. John hoped it would prove impossible to collect Richard's ransom, that he himself could hire mercenaries from Wales and Scotland, raise troops from his honours and castles in England and then proclaim himself King, while Philip's army would help him to lay hold of the rest of the Angevin empire. But once again John was thwarted. His mother, now a formidable old lady of seventy who had returned to England after accompanying Richard to Sicily, rallied troops on behalf of her elder son and even obliged John to conclude a truce; and the majority of the barons remained loyal to the regency of Walter de Coutances. De Coutances raised the money needed for the ransom and took it to Germany. When he received the news of his brother's projected release, John fled

RIGHT Richard I as a prisoner at the Court of Duke Leopold of Austria. The Duke, a bitter enemy of Richard, handed him over to the Emperor Henry VI for a substantial fee. Richard was held captive for a year and ransomed for 150,000 marks.

OPPOSITE Château-Gaillard on the island of Andeli in the Seine, built by Richard I in 1196 to guard the approaches to Rouen.

LEFT Medieval builders from a mid-thirteenth-century manuscript. The illustration shows various aspects of building, including the line and plummet level; a windlass and basket; a plumb-line and mortar bowl; carving an Early English capital; and a carpenter with an adze.

back to France, whereupon his castles in England were taken over by the regency, now headed by Hubert Walter, Arch-bishop of Canterbury. In March 1194 Richard at last returned to England and John skulked in Normandy fearing the worst; for he had, after all, been an open rebel, a traitor to his liege lord.

After his return to England King Richard seized his brother's most important castle at Nottingham and summoned John to appear before his Court within forty days in order to undergo judgment as a rebel. Richard then had himself recrowned at Winchester and soon set sail for Normandy where Philip II was besieging the frontier castles. On his way Richard heard that John was at Lisieux. The King ordered his younger brother to appear before him after sending him a promise of mercy. When John threw himself at his brother's feet, Richard proved him-self magnanimous or contemptuous. Addressed as 'a naughty child', John (who was then twenty-seven) was stripped of all his possessions and titles except that of Lord of Ireland and was for-bidden to hold any more castles in England. During the cam-paign in Normandy John fought loyally beside his brother. The war was a long one and punctuated by truce and treaty. By the treaty of Louviers in 1195 Richard yielded the Norman Vexin to Philip, but then proceeded to build the impressive castle known as Château-Gaillard at a bend in the River Seine. The castle had in addition to its stone keep both an inner and an

31

The castle of Chinon in Touraine, one of
the most vital of the Angevin fortresses:
it was here that King Henry II died.

outer bailey (or defensive enclosures) protected with moats. Possibly it was the strongest and most up-to-date castle in Europe. It served a dual purpose, for it covered Rouen, the Norman capital, and could be used as a springboard from which to recapture the surrendered Vexin.

During these years which he spent mostly with his brother, John must have learned much of the arts of war and diplomacy including how to hold, defend and attack castles. Richard was able to conclude treaties of alliance with the Counts of Flanders and Boulogne, whose territories had been subjected to English economic pressure. One of Richard's brothers-in-law was King of Navarre and another Count of Toulouse. Thus both the northern and southern flanks of Richard's territories in France were secured by friendly neighbours. In Richard's last battle with Philip II, fought at Gisors, the strength of his charge so shook the French King that he and many of his knights had the bridge into the town broken underneath them and fell into the river Epte.

John's services in these campaigns gradually restored him to his brother's favour and in 1195 he was reinstated as Count of Mortain and Earl of Gloucester. Early in April 1199 Richard was killed at the age of forty-one in an obscure side-show. Negligently besieging the castle of a vassal in the Limousin, who refused to hand over to him some ancient treasure that he had found, Richard did not put on his armour: a wound that he received during the conflict festered and the King died. Before he did so, he is believed to have named John as his heir.

John took speedy action to secure his inheritance. As it happened, John was not with his brother when he expired on 6 April, but was in Brittany staying with his nephew Arthur and Arthur's mother Constance (the loquacious character in Shakespeare's play *King John*). When he heard the news, John promptly rode into Touraine to seize the treasury at Chinon. From Chinon he went on to his brother's funeral at the abbey of Fontevrault where Richard was buried beside his father. Then John rode on to Le Mans in Maine. But there he was coldly received and found that Philip II's army and Arthur of Brittany's partisans were already converging on the town. He made good his escape to Normandy where on 25 April he was acclaimed Duke at Rouen. Later he led a Norman army back to Le Mans,

Detail from the tomb of
Hubert Walter,
Archbishop of Canterbury
from 1189 to 1205, in
Canterbury Cathedral.

imprisoned the leading citizens of the town and levelled its
castle and walls to the ground as punishment for their defiance
of him.

Meanwhile the question of who ought to succeed to the
English throne was under discussion. Hubert Walter, the Archbishop of Canterbury, and William Marshal, the future Earl of
Pembroke, both ripely experienced statesmen, happened to be
together in Normandy at the time. The problem was a tricky
one. The Archbishop took a gloomy view: 'The King', he said,
'is dead. What hope remains to us now? There is none, for,
after him, I can see no successor able to defend the kingdom.'
The Archbishop at first favoured Arthur, but William Marshal
emphatically advocated John. He argued that Arthur of Brit-

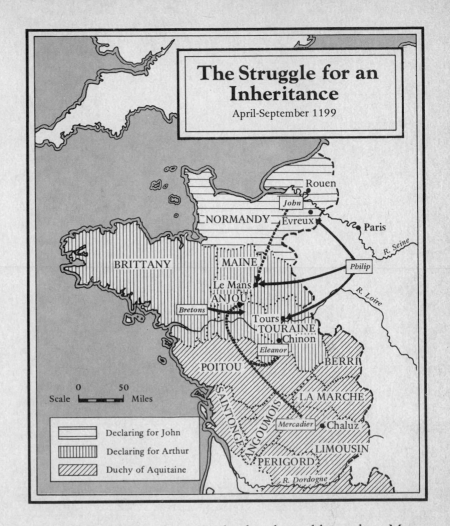

Rouen

John

NORMANDY
Evreux

Paris

R. Seine

BRITTANY

MAINE

Philip

Le Mans
ANJOU

R. Loire

Bretons

Tours
TOURAINE
Chinon

Eleanor

BERRI

POITOU

Scale 0   50   Miles

LA MARCHE

AINTONGE

ANGOUMOIS

Mercadier   Chaluz

LIMOUSIN

PERIGORD

R. Dordogne

	Declaring for John
	Declaring for Arthur
	Duchy of Aquitaine

OPPOSITE The tomb of William Marshal, Earl of Pembroke, in the Temple Church, London. Marshal helped John to obtain the throne in 1199 and was one of his most able supporters throughout the reign. He was one of the great lords who remained faithful to the King during the rebellion of 1215–16 and he helped to secure the succession of Henry III in 1216.

tany knew nothing about England and would care less. Moreover, he asserted that the law preferred a younger brother to the son of an elder brother. That in fact was doubtful. But Marshal also considered that John was the abler man and had far more experience. So the two magnates came to an agreement and hurried over to England to persuade Geoffrey fitz Peter, Earl of Essex, who had succeeded Hubert Walter as Chief Justiciar in 1198, to side with them. A fortnight after this conversation John landed at Shoreham from Dieppe, having left his immediate problems in central France in the capable hands of his mother and his late brother's mercenaries. Two days later, on the feast of the Ascension, John was crowned King of England in Westminster Abbey.

The Loss of Normandy 1199-1204

JOHN'S ACCESSION TO POWER had been peacefully received in both England and Normandy. In Aquitaine Queen Eleanor resumed her rights as duchess and did immediate homage to King Philip II at Tours, but later handed over authority to John. The chief threat to John's position in France appeared to come from Brittany, Anjou and Maine, where the claims of Arthur to succeed his uncle Richard were being pressed. But in fact the greatest danger was from King Philip whose statesmanship was so outstanding that he was called Augustus after the Roman Emperor. Philip was known to be anxious to extend his territorial possessions instead of being merely the overlord of the Angevins. He was still occupied in military operations along the frontier of Normandy after John's coronation. The intricacies of feudal law offered many excuses for Philip Augustus to wage war on John, if he wished to do so.

But the French King was not yet ready to strike. His long and unavailing struggle with Richard I had made inroads into his resources, while he was also in conflict with the Papacy because he had taken a third wife without properly getting rid of his second wife. He therefore bided his time, but he did not conceal his ambitions. Negotiations were opened between Philip and John at the beginning of 1200. Before that John had come to terms with Arthur of Brittany and his mother. John accepted Arthur's homage for the duchy. He was also reconciled to Arthur's mother and it did not look as if the young man would cause any more trouble to his uncle John.

On 22 May 1200 a treaty was agreed between Philip and John at Le Goulet on the River Seine. By its terms Philip accepted John as the rightful heir to all the fiefs that Richard had held in France. In return John granted a number of important concessions. First, he undertook to pay Philip the substantial sum of 20,000 marks as a relief, that is to say by way of a succession duty; secondly, he allowed Philip to retain a number of disputed fiefs on the frontier of Normandy including the Vexin (apart from the island of Andeli on which the newly-built castle of Château-Gaillard stood) and the county of Evreux; thirdly, it was arranged that Blanche, John's niece by his sister Eleanor, who had married the King of Castile, should be betrothed to Philip's heir, Louis, and should receive as her dowry valuable lordships in Berri. Philip recognised that John was

PREVIOUS PAGES Battle scene from *Le Estoire de St Aedward*.

40

Seal of Philip Augustus, King of France
from 1180 to 1223. Under his able leadership the French
won control over most of the Angevin 'empire'.

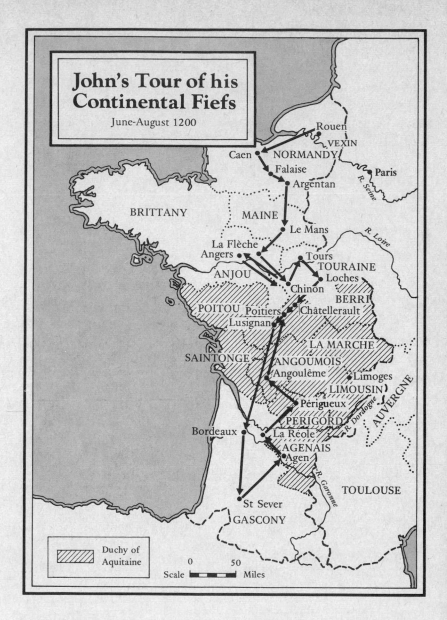

John's Tour of his Continental Fiefs

June-August 1200

Duchy of
Aquitaine

0   50
Scale ━━━━━━ Miles

Arthur's overlord and John accepted that the Counts of Boulogne and Flanders, who had been traditional allies of England,
'are or ought to be rather the vassals of the French King than of
us'. On the face of it this was a statesmanlike treaty in which
each side yielded concessions in return for positive gains. But
in it, of course, as is the case with most treaties, were the seeds of
future disputes. It was said by some people in England that
neither Henry II nor Richard I would have given away so much

and John received, rather unfairly, the nickname of 'Softsword'.

After he had agreed to the treaty John spent three months touring his Continental fiefs. Among the most sensitive areas in his domain were the counties of Lusignan, La Marche, Angoulême and Limoges, which linked Poitou, the northern part of Aquitaine, with Gascony in the south. Richard had experienced his difficulties with the rebellious independence of the barons in that area. John thought up a brilliant idea. Why should he not pacify them by marriage? His first wife, Isabella of Gloucester, had borne him no children and had taken no part in his coronation. Whether by accident or design, papal approval had never been obtained during the long years after John's marriage to his second cousin, thus violating the 'prohibited degrees'. John had no difficulty in finding a couple of bishops to pronounce that his first marriage was invalid. On 24 August 1200 John was able to marry Isabelle, daughter of Count Audemar of Angoulême in Aquitaine.

The medieval chroniclers, mostly looking back in the light of future events, wove a romantic story around John's marriage to Isabelle of Angoulême. They said that he had fallen in love with her and that because she had previously been engaged to her father's neighbour and rival, the widowed Hugh IX, Lord of Lusignan and Count of La Marche, the angry Lusignans had appealed to King Philip II for vengeance, thus bringing about the loss of Normandy to John. There is no basis for this legend. Isabelle is variously estimated to have been eleven, twelve, thirteen or fourteen at the time. John had plenty of mistresses and it is highly unlikely that he fell in love so opportunely with this particular child. The Lusignans did not appeal to Philip Augustus against John until some eighteen months after the marriage had taken place and King John had found another wife for Hugh IX in a ward of his own named Matilda. By then Hugh IX's brother Ralph, who held a fief, Eu, in eastern Normandy, had been roughly treated by John and threatened with the confiscation of his county. Thus the Lusignans had bigger grievances against John than the rupture of an engagement. In fact John's marriage was one of convenience. It 'made very good political sense' and 'healed a running sore' (W.L. Warren). Count Audemar not only ruled Angoulême but had claims to La Marche and was the half-brother of the Count of

Effigy of Isabelle of Angoulême, John's second wife and the mother of Henry III, from her tomb at Fontevrault. John married her in 1200, his first marriage having been declared invalid.

Limoges. John could therefore hope to win influential friends in a vital strategic area, while by the terms of the marriage settlement he himself would become Count of Angoulême when his father-in-law died.

In October John returned with his bride to England and they were crowned together in Westminster Abbey, although John was not anointed, since he had been crowned already. Then he devoted the next six months to travelling round England, just as previously he had toured his lands in France. At Lincoln in November he met the King of the Scots, known as William the Lion, who came to pay homage to his new overlord and optimistically but unsuccessfully asked that the counties of Northumberland, Cumberland and Westmorland should be joined to his dominions. In February 1201 John and his new Queen visited York where the King was reconciled to his half-brother, Geoffrey, Archbishop of York, with whom he had been on extremely bad terms chiefly because of questions of money. The King and Queen spent Easter at Canterbury where they 'wore their crowns', Hubert Walter as Archbishop performing the ceremony at the feast.

Meanwhile troubles were piling up for John in France. Queen Eleanor wrote her son agitated letters from Aquitaine. The Lusignans, she said, were becoming turbulent, perhaps because they hoped that John would compensate them more generously for his marriage *coup* in Angoulême, but had failed to do so. John instructed his officials to take over Hugh's county of La Marche and to harry Ralph by seizing his castle of Drincourt. At Easter John ordered his English vassals to gather in Portsmouth during Whitsuntide ready for a campaign in France. Whether he changed his mind about this or not is uncertain, but at any rate he did not, after all, take his English feudal host to France with him; instead he collected money from the knights assembled at Portsmouth and used it to hire mercenaries. At the end of May 1201 he landed in Normandy.

There John was greeted by his overlord, Philip Augustus, who was not yet anxious to disturb the peace established by the treaty of Le Goulet. He therefore told the Lusignans to behave themselves and invited the English King to pay a State visit to Paris where he was magnificently entertained. Everything seemed to be going swimmingly for John. He patched up a

OPPOSITE Anointing a king at his coronation, an illustration from the thirteenth-century Maciesowski Psalter.

Medieval Warfare

Warfare, both private and
public, played a large
part in medieval history.
A king was judged, above
all, on the basis of his
military achievements,
and one of the reasons why
John acquired a bad
reputation was that he lost
most of the Angevin lands
in France. As well as
kings, earls and barons
assessed their strength by
the number of
knights they could put
into the field.

RIGHT ABOVE A knight
getting into a suit of
armour, with a knight and
king, fully-armed, on
horseback; from a
thirteenth-century
manuscript.
RIGHT Attacking a castle
gate with axe and
spear. The huge curved
shields, held above the
attackers' heads, protect
them from the missiles
being thrown from the
castle walls.

uatr dauit uemeno i castra cum offere uellet que attulerat. audito clamore acierum que
ad pugnam parate erant dimittit omnia ad sarcinas custorum sub manu custodis q ipe
aperant uadit ad locum prelij ~

qualiter cum dauit uenisz ad locum errauuius er ille gigas more solito expiraret. atq ois
Isrsl cum ualde timeret. unus dixit q quicuq illu post occdere. rex ei filiam suam cu ducusz
multis daret. atq cum et oem domu patris sui imunem faceret a tributo. qd audiens dauit.
er de conditionibz illr diligenter interrogans: cum omnia didicissz contempsit illum gigantem q
de uictoria se habere optimam spem ostendit. fratres eu sui grauiter increpuerunt.

وذکره ازانله نذعادی برببان اسکر برامد و دستام میداد و کسی نفرمود ، باوت دسناوی
کهمکودغ اين اوی کند و اوراکتبار اوشاه دخترخودرا مال سیار ولعمت ینثار به اوارزند میدارد و ینفاماله ولطف
میمود ازان لبین سرپنداشت کنفت منزمیروانرااحاسبرکنتمداداش منع کرونداندتو ازانبانی که

LEFT Scenes of a campaign from the Maciesowski Psalter. The upper section shows a baggage wagon filled with clothes and armour, with cooking pots hanging on the outside.

RIGHT Knights entering a city, from a fourteenth-century manuscript.
RIGHT BELOW A ballista, a medieval engine used for hurling stones; an illustration from the fourteenth-century Flemish manuscript, the Romance of Alexander.

A king and queen feasting.

peace with the Count of Eu and assured Philip that he would do
justice by his vassals. His former enemy Constance of Brittany
died in August of that year and he saw to the carrying out of her
last wishes. He settled a generous dowry on Richard I's widow,
Berengaria of Navarre, and he then negotiated an alliance with
her brother, King Sancho VII. But Nemesis followed Hubris.
Overcome by his good fortune, John was careless in his handling
of the touchy Lusignans. Instead of summoning them to his
Court to discuss their grievances, he charged them with treason
and invited them to prove their innocence by fighting a judicial
duel with professional champions named by him. Understandably the Lusignans refused and appealed to John's overlord
for justice. John continued to follow a strong line and by the
spring of 1202 he had both laid hold of the castle of Drincourt
and ordered that Ralph should be deprived of his county of Eu.

Philip Augustus's patience was now exhausted and he
decided upon a show-down with King John. He asserted that
John had failed to give a fair trial to the Lusignan brothers as he
had promised to do. He demanded that John should surrender

three Norman castles to him as an earnest of good behaviour and required John to appear before his Court in Paris a fortnight after Easter to defend himself. John refused to comply on the ground that as Duke of Normandy he was not obliged to treat with his overlord anywhere except on the borders of his duchy. Philip retorted that John was not being summoned in his capacity of Duke of Normandy but as Duke of Aquitaine. Thus an impasse was reached. John refused to surrender any castles or to go to Paris. According to one of the more reliable chroniclers, Ralph of Coggeshall, Philip's Court now found John guilty of contumacy and sentenced him to the forfeiture of all the lands he held of the French Crown. Whether that is true or not, negotiations broke down between the two Kings; and early in May war began with a raid by Philip II on one of the Norman frontier castles which he captured and destroyed.

John was to spend much of his reign fighting either to hold

or to regain his possessions in France, to secure his frontiers or 'marches' in England, and to overcome rebels in civil war. It is therefore necessary to understand the nature of medieval warfare. In battle the mounted knights, who wore chain armour and wielded a sword, spear and shield, could play a decisive part and were also useful for protecting columns of infantry on the march or for raiding. If a knight wore his armour and helmet he was virtually impossible to kill, although when he fell off his horse he found it hard to get up again: he needed a squire to help him remount. But set battles were few and far between. Most of the warfare consisted of attacking or defending castles and for that purpose the mounted and armoured knight was not essential.

Castles such as had been built by the early Norman kings out of earth and timber, known as motte-and-bailey castles, had now been largely superseded by keep-and-bailey castles with

thick stone walls and a stone keep, which was often the residence of a baron and was capable of separate defence. The tower keep (or *turris*) was a massive rectangular building, which was hard to capture, but the baileys beside or beneath the keep were also usually protected by stone walls as well as ditches and earthen ramparts. Most castles were royal or ducal. A licence was required for the erection of a private castle, and the king or duke could demand the right of entry in time of war. The castles could best be defended by crossbowmen and the only ways in which they could be attacked were by mining or by stone-throwing engines. Mining could be met with counter-mining (though that was a dangerous practice) but if the castle were built upon rock it could not be mined. The stone-throwing siege weapons – the best known were mangonels and trébuchets – were employed to batter a breach in the walls through which an assault might be undertaken. But if the castles were really strong – for example, if they were cylindrical in shape or so constructed that the garrison could move from one part to another through a curtain wall – they were extremely hard to overcome. In fact it was one of those periods in the history of war when a determined defensive could hope to obtain complete mastery over the offensive.

Though knights were used to take command or to act as constables of castles, the Angevin kings preferred to exact scutage with which to hire mercenaries rather than to rely on a whole host of knights who were unlikely to be highly trained or disciplined. The knight would be paid eightpence a day, and forty times eightpence (forty days was the time a knight was required to serve abroad) would buy a lot of mercenaries. The mercenaries varied in quality from younger sons of the nobility to the scum of Flemish towns. Knights (*milites*) and sergeants (*servientes*) might also be hired and paid for with either money or gifts of land. They could be light cavalrymen, crossbowmen or pikemen. But the pikemen were only useful in defence.

Wars were generally fought according to set rules. It was not done to fight in the winter and short truces were common. Before a campaign began, consideration was given to the question whether some agreement might not be concluded between the two sides. If it could not, fighting would start in the spring and cease when the harvest was due to be gathered.

Preparing food and taking it to the table in the house of a great lord.

If a castle was surrounded and cut off, a truce would be agreed between the assailants and the defenders during which the garrison made up its mind whether or not a relief force was likely to arrive. If its supplies were low and no help was forthcoming within a given time, the defenders would then submit to honourable capitulation. Much of the fighting in King John's reign therefore was done by mercenaries, who were more proficient than the feudal host, and took place among rings of castles which protected the frontiers of Normandy and Brittany, just as they did the frontiers of Scotland and Wales. John himself was no mean soldier – some think that he was quite as good as his brother and better than his father – and was to have striking victories to his credit. His defeats were due more to lack of resources, which was a natural consequence of the extravagances of his brother's reign, and to the intransigence of his barons both in France and in England, rather than to any personal deficiences. He had mastered the art of war when serving with Richard I and was neither unintelligent nor cowardly.

The grievances of the Lusignans were only the excuse used by Philip Augustus to drive John out of Normandy. Immediately after John's condemnation by the Court in Paris the French King attacked northern Normandy down the line of the Seine and methodically captured castles, starting with Boutevant and Gournai, and then laid siege to Arques, which protected access to the seaport of Dieppe. At the end of July 1202 King Philip knighted Arthur of Brittany and received his homage for Brittany, Poitou, Anjou, Maine and Touraine. But significantly Philip did not recognise Arthur's claim to Normandy: for he intended that it should become an integral part of France.

Meanwhile John was not idle; he sent Hubert Walter to England to tell his leading subjects and officials there about the unjustified and unprovoked attack that had been launched upon his French inheritance. After collecting money and recruits, he prepared to defend southern Normandy. He took up head-quarters at Le Mans in Maine from which he could keep watch over events both in Normandy and in Aquitaine. On 30 July he learned that Arthur, with a force of knights including two of the Lusignans, was besieging Mirebeau, a town in Anjou to the north-west of Poitiers, which was being gallantly defended by

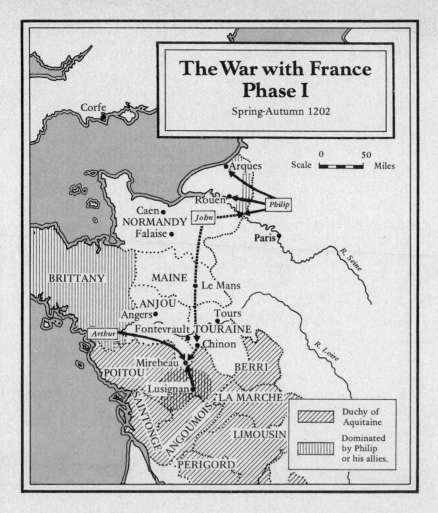

Scale 0 50 Miles

Corfe

Arques

Rouen
Philip

Caen
NORMANDY
Falaise *John*

Paris

R. Seine

BRITTANY

MAINE
Le Mans

ANJOU
Angers
Tours
Fontevrault TOURAINE
Arthur
Chinon

R. Loire

Mirebeau
BERRI
POITOU
Lusignan
LA MARCHE
SAINTONGE
ANGOUMOIS
LIMOUSIN
PERIGORD

Duchy of
Aquitaine

Dominated
by Philip
or his allies.

John's aged mother from the keep. John made a forced march
from Le Mans across the River Loire and surprised the besiegers
in the narrow streets of Mirebeau during the early morning of
1 August. William des Roches, the seneschal of Anjou and
Maine, led the successful attack. One of John's companions,
William de Braose, took Arthur of Brittany a prisoner and
handed him over to the King. Two of the Lusignans, Hugh IX
and his uncle Geoffrey, were also captured. Arthur and the
Lusignans were sent to Falaise in Normandy, other prisoners to
Corfe Castle in Dorset. The news of this remarkable victory
shook Philip Augustus who immediately abandoned the siege
of Arques, ravaging the borders of Normandy as he retired.
John followed up his triumph by occupying Tours and Angers

57

Medieval Castles

In medieval times castles served both as fortresses from which to control the surrounding land, and as places of residence for lords. The twelfth and thirteenth centuries were great centuries of English castle building, the early Norman motte-and-bailey castles being gradually replaced by keep-and-bailey castles, with thick stone walls and a stone keep.

LEFT Orford Castle in Suffolk,
built between 1165 and 1173
by Henry II.
ABOVE Castle Rising in Norfolk.
The keep is an excellent example
of early Norman work.
RIGHT Ruins of the keep of
Corfe Castle, destroyed in the
civil war in the seventeenth century.
It was considered one of the safest
strategic fortresses and prisons
in southern England at the time
of King John.

as well as Le Mans. But so fierce had the war become that the usual truce at harvest time was not agreed to, and fighting continued into the winter.

All might have gone well with John had he not quarrelled with his victorious general, William des Roches. It was not altogether surprising that he did so. William des Roches, the most powerful baron in Anjou, had previously been 'the right hand of Constance and Arthur' and had been recognised as Constable in Anjou, Maine and Touraine by King Philip II. He had deserted to John's side when he perceived the trend of events at the outset of John's reign. A man of devouring ambition, he had clearly grown too big for his boots after the victory at Mirebeau and had demanded that the fate of Arthur of Brittany should be settled by him. John refused to be dictated to, ignored his advice and removed him from his office of seneschal. William des Roches retorted by occupying Angers while another dissident baron seized Tours. At the same time the Bretons, agitated over the fate of Duke Arthur, who had been a heroic figure to them, were making ready to enter the war against John. Thus by the time John was spending Christmas in some comfort at Caen in Normandy, the outlook for the next campaign was beginning to appear less bright. An attempt to come to terms with King Philip led nowhere.

John now tried to strengthen his position in France by two drastic actions. First, he made an arrangement with his prisoner, Hugh IX of Lusignan, allowing him to buy his freedom. That was a sensible decision because if John could reach a friendly agreement with the Lusignans, when he succeeded his father-in-law as Count of Angoulême (which he did in 1202) he could hope to secure the vital areas in central France which commanded the roads between Poitou and Gascony. Secondly, John had his rival, Arthur of Brittany, put to death. The widely accepted story of Arthur's fate – which differs from that portrayed in Shakespeare's play – is exceedingly dramatic, though it depends upon how much credibility can be attached to accounts recorded by monastic chroniclers writing well after the event. The story is first that John was persuaded that his nephew should be blinded and castrated, but that the order which he gave that this should be done was disobeyed by Hubert de Burgh, the baron who had charge of Arthur in Falaise.

61

Subsequently Arthur, it is said, was removed to Rouen, the capital of Normandy, and there on 3 April 1203 was put to death. A monastic chronicler in the Cistercian abbey of Margam in Glamorgan gives a circumstantial description of Arthur of Brittany's end:

> After King John had captured Arthur and kept him alive in prison for some time, at length in the castle of Rouen after dinner on the Thursday before Easter when he was drunk and possessed by the Devil, he slew him with his own hand, and tying a heavy stone to the body cast it into the Seine. It was discovered by a fisherman in his net, and being dragged to the bank and recognised, was taken for secret burial ...

The main reason for crediting this tale is that William de Braose, who had actually taken Arthur prisoner, is known to have been a patron of the Margam monastery and might have been aware of what had happened and told it to the monks; it can also be argued that the story is too elaborate to have been made up. A reference in a letter, written by John to his mother and others on 16 April 1203, in which he says that 'God's Grace had stood him in better stead than he could possibly indicate', has been interpreted to refer to the death of Arthur on 3 April. Another chronicler, writing after John's death, recorded that Arthur had been 'shamefully murdered'. But a statement that the French Court solemnly condemned John for murdering his nephew has never been fully substantiated. A number of distinguished historians, however, have considered that the Margam chronicler's account is highly probable.

The execution by the head of State of a rival who could become the focus of an opposition is a commonplace in the history of Europe. King Henry IV had Richard II executed; Edward IV had Henry VI executed; Richard III had his nephew Edward V put to death in the Tower of London; Queen Elizabeth I caused Mary Queen of Scots to lose her head; Stalin disposed of his rivals in Soviet Russia by summary trial. Duke Arthur of Brittany had waged war against his uncle whom three years earlier he had acknowledged as his overlord. The great Pope Innocent III thought that John was entirely justified in putting Arthur to death without trial as a traitor. That John killed Arthur with his own hands in a drunken fury may be believed by some modern biographers; but such a melodramatic

'He slew him with his own hand'

PREVIOUS PAGES
A magnificent battle scene from the Maciesowski Psalter. On the edge of the picture is a slinging machine, the weighted end of which is being pulled down to jerk the stone from the sling into the city.

64

story would certainly not be regarded as proven in an impartial modern court of law.

When the war was renewed in the spring of 1203 the military situation rapidly deteriorated for King John. King Philip resumed his attacks on the outer defences of Normandy; in Poitou barons broke into rebellion; and the Bretons, distressed by the death or disappearance of their hero, Arthur, assaulted Normandy from the west. Under such pressure John found it difficult to organise a counter-offensive and he moved uncertainly between Argentan in south-western Normandy and the capital, Rouen, which was also his principal magazine. At the end of August Philip II laid siege to Château-Gaillard, the mighty fortress built by Richard I to protect Rouen. John was confident that the English Constable, Roger de Lacy, would be able to defend it indefinitely so long as he was not starved out. The English King planned a combined operation to relieve the castle. While supplies were rowed up the Seine in seventy boats, guarded by a naval detachment, William Marshal was to lead an armed contingent up the left bank of the river to surprise the French encampment. It was a plan worthy of Richard I. However, the naval and land forces were unable to synchronise their advance and William Marshal's men were routed. After the failure of his imaginative scheme at Château-Gaillard John turned his attention to the Bretons, sacked the town of Dol and set its cathedral on fire. But Philip could not be distracted from his campaign in Normandy. John realising that the Norman barons were no longer loyal to him – castles had been treasonably surrendered to the French, decided to return to England at the beginning of December and ask help from his barons there.

John and his Queen spent Christmas in Canterbury and in January 1204 John summoned a council of his barons to meet in Oxford. There they voted him a substantial sum of money (two-and-a-half marks for each knight's fee) and John prepared to return to Normandy. But early in March the dreadful news arrived that the apparently impregnable Château-Gaillard had fallen, not through starvation or treachery, but to a direct assault engineered by siege machines and mining. The French King resolved not to attack Rouen at once but to march into western Normandy and there join hands with the Bretons. In the early summer Philip took the historic towns of Falaise and

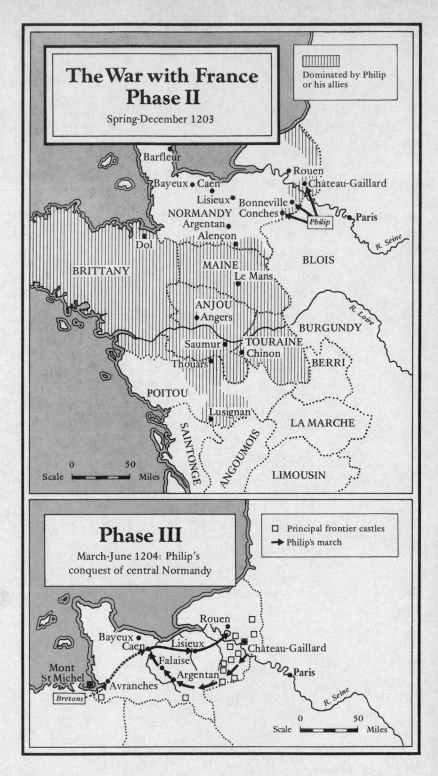

The War with France
Phase II

Spring–December 1203

Dominated by Philip or his allies

Barfleur

Rouen
Château-Gaillard

Bayeux • Caen

Lisieux
Bonneville
NORMANDY   Conches
Argentan
Philip   Paris

Alençon

Dol

BLOIS

R. Seine

BRITTANY   MAINE
Le Mans

ANJOU   R. Loire
Angers

BURGUNDY

Saumur   TOURAINE
Thouars   Chinon
BERRI

POITOU

Lusignan
LA MARCHE

Scale   0   50   Miles

SAINTONGE

ANGOUMOIS   LIMOUSIN

Phase III

March–June 1204: Philip's conquest of central Normandy

☐ Principal frontier castles
→ Philip's march

Rouen

Bayeux • Caen
Lisieux   Château-Gaillard
Falaise
Argentan   Paris
Mont St Michel
Bretons   Avranches   R. Seine

Scale   0   50   Miles

66

Caen, while the Bretons broke through Mont St Michel and occupied Avranches. Thus the whole of Normandy was overrun by John's enemies, except for Rouen, which was isolated. On 1 June the commander at Rouen arranged with Philip that, if John did not come to his rescue within thirty days, he would surrender. In fact Philip was admitted to the city on 24 June 1204. So John lost the whole of Normandy (except the Channel Islands).

Why was Normandy lost and how far was John himself to blame? Undoubtedly the Normans did not respect John's military reputation as much as they had done that of Richard. But it is doubtful if Richard, had he still been alive, would have been able to save Normandy, though he might perhaps have died heroically in defence of Rouen. But the Normans had long been tiring of Angevin rule and the barons there were attracted by the delights of Paris rather than those of London. They had been alienated by the ruthlessness of King Richard and angered at the devastation caused by King John's mercenaries. It was even suggested by the contemporary Gerald of Wales that the Normans, who had been harshly downtrodden, preferred not to resist 'the fierce courage of free Frenchmen'. Perhaps more to the point was the military consideration that while John had to disperse his resources and energies throughout the whole huge 'Angevin empire', Philip Augustus was able to concentrate his army on the southern frontier of Normandy and break through the ring of castles there, since few natural defences existed, the rivers helping rather than hindering the invaders. Thus John personally can be blamed only to a minor degree for the loss of Normandy. As Professor Warren has written: 'It is difficult to see how John could have averted disaster. Not even the ablest commander can hold a disaffected province indefinitely against a determined invader.'

'The fierce courage of free Frenchmen'

SOMETHING LIKE PANIC gripped King John and his Court following the loss of Normandy which the French King now took over completely as part of his dominions. Might John's defeat there foreshadow the disintegration of the entire Angevin empire in France? In the spring of 1204 John dispatched a powerful embassy, including Hubert Walter and William Marshal, to try to open negotiations with Philip II. Philip asked that Arthur of Brittany, whom he must have suspected was dead, should be handed over to him in order that the Duke might do homage for the remaining possessions of the House of Anjou in France. So the mission was abortive. Furthermore Philip required that English barons who held lands in Normandy, such as William Marshal, should do homage to him for them. John answered by confiscating lands held by Norman barons in England, though these were not extensive. In the course of the summer of 1205 the castles of Chinon and Loches, both in Touraine, fell into the hands of the French and their allies. Once again William Marshal went on a peace mission to the French King, having obtained from John permission – or at least that is what he thought – to do homage for his lands in Normandy. But again nothing came of the negotiations; Hubert Walter, who was opposed to any complete surrender by King John, sent a secret message to Philip II telling him that Marshal had no authority to conclude peace.

It was bad enough for an Angevin king to have to accept, at any rate for the time being, the loss of Normandy, Brittany, Anjou, Maine and Touraine, but might he not have to forfeit also his mother's duchy of Aquitaine (the old lady was now at last dead) if he did not return to fight in France? At the outset of 1205 an even graver danger faced King John. Philip Augustus was known to be contemplating the invasion of England. In February the French King held a meeting at Vernon in Normandy with the Count of Boulogne and the Duke of Brabant, formerly John's allies. Not for the first nor last time an attack upon England across the Channel was planned. So John had to concentrate on home defence. The kingdom was divided into a vast 'commune' in which every male over the age of twelve had to bear arms. This huge militia was allocated to the command of constables in the shires, the hundreds (sub-divisions of the shires) and the towns. By a writ issued in

The manufacture of weapons:
ABOVE LEFT Edging up a sword.
ABOVE RIGHT Grinding a sword on
a large and heavy wheel.
BELOW Hammering a helmet. One of the
smiths is squinting down a sword to test it.

April 1205 every nine knights in the kingdom were required to equip and pay a tenth knight to stand ready to defend the realm. But if the invasion materialised then every knight would be required to take up arms. In May a scheme which John had worked out for a pincer movement against the French with one army landing in Normandy and another in Aquitaine had to be abandoned even though a military host was assembled at Northampton and a fleet of ships at Portsmouth. Hubert Walter and William Marshal joined forces to persuade the King that it was dangerous to send troops out of England at such a critical time. John was angry with frustration but acquiesced. So the bulk of the expeditionary force intended for France stayed in England. Philip II then gave up his plan for invasion and instead sent his soldiers to mop up in Touraine and Poitou.

Once the danger of invasion had passed in the summer of 1205 John resolved to reassert his authority in Aquitaine. In June 1206 he landed at La Rochelle and led his army into Gascony where he captured the strategic castle of Mountauban, situated at the junction of the rivers Dordogne and Garonne, which was in the hands of rebels. John battered the castle into submission with siege engines and took many valuable prisoners. Then he turned back north and, joined by some of the Poitevin barons, crossed the Loire and retook Angers in Anjou. But the Poitevins were not prepared to fight against their overlord, the King of France, and on 26 October a two-year truce was concluded on the basis of the *status quo*. Thus John had preserved much of his mother's inheritance and might hope in time to marshal his resources so as to resume war against Philip in order to regain Normandy, Brittany, Maine, Anjou and Touraine.

During the first years of his reign, while he was engaged in war in France, John owed much for the peace and stability that prevailed in England and also for his ability to collect money to pay for his army and navy to the devoted services of the statesmen whom he had inherited from his brother, such as Hubert Walter, appointed Chancellor in May 1199 in addition to being Archbishop of Canterbury, Geoffrey fitz Peter, the Justiciar, and William, Earl of Pembroke, the Marshal of his household. John was a capable and energetic administrator himself but he needed reliable servants. It has been seen how it was the influence of Walter and Marshal which had originally

forbidden by the canons of the Church; and that he was an indifferent preacher. But as a politician he gave value for money. He acted as a mediator between the Church and the Angevin kings. He protected both Cistercian monks in England and other monks in Poitou against John's exactions. On one occasion John begged Hubert's forgiveness with tears in his eyes for having offended the Church. When on 13 July 1205 Hubert Walter died, John lost an invaluable adviser. As John was alienated from William Marshal when the Earl paid homage to Philip Augustus for his possessions in Normandy, he was left without two of his most experienced counsellors at a critical point in his reign. It may well be that some of the mistakes that the King then made were largely owing to this loss.

The question of who was to succeed Hubert Walter as Archbishop of Canterbury was to have profound consequences for the remainder of John's reign. The relations between State and Church or between the King and his leading archbishop had been fraught with difficulties ever since the time of William the Conqueror. William I had deposed the Anglo-Saxon

The martyrdom of Thomas Becket. The scene on the left shows Henry II demanding of his knights why no one will rid him of the troublesome 'clerk'. On the right the four knights are shown murdering Becket in Canterbury Cathedral.

Archbishop Stigand; William II had left the archbishopric vacant for some years and then quarrelled with his own appointee, Archbishop Anselm. Henry I had his troubles with Anselm, and Henry II with Archbishop Thomas Becket. Archbishops and bishops were not merely princes of the Church but were also magnates, tenants-in-chief, ecclesiastical barons and generally ministers or advisers of the Crown. It was therefore in the interest of the King to see that compliant or at any rate agreeable men should become bishops; on the other hand, reforming Popes and the canonists of the Church were anxious to ensure that devout and practising Christians should occupy the bishops' sees.

Innocent III, who became Pope in 1198 at the remarkably early age of thirty-seven, was particularly emphatic about the need for bishops to be men of the highest character, learned and knowledgeable. Indeed he insisted upon this throughout the whole of Europe wherever he was recognised as head of the Roman Church. Innocent was a dynamic personality and a fine preacher, but he was also a diplomatist and opportunist who

wanted to rally the European monarchs to set out upon a Fourth Crusade. Under him 'the religious life of Western Europe was organised and directed as never before' (E.F. Jacob). Thus the question of who was to be appointed the spiritual head of the Church in England was a matter of much moment to him.

Canon laws and precedents in regard to the appointments of English bishops were by no means crystal clear. By what was known as the Compromise of Bec, concluded between King Henry I and Archbishop Anselm in 1106, the cathedral chapters had the authority freely to elect bishops, but the elections were subject to the King's right to influence nominations and to veto appointments. By the Constitutions of Clarendon (1164), in which King Henry II aimed to define the relationship between Church and State in England, it was laid down (Clause XII) that the election of bishops should take place in the royal chapel and should be subject to the approval of the King and his Council. Thus even though the elections did not take place in the royal chapel in John's reign, the 'free election' had become rather a farce and in effect bishops were chosen by the King as they had been in Anglo-Saxon times.

When Hubert Walter died, John was determined that his secretary, John de Gray, Bishop of Norwich, should fill the vacancy. But as there was some argument in Canterbury about who had the right to elect the primate – the monks of the chapter alone or the bishops of the province as well – John ordered that the election should be postponed until December 1205 so that the Papacy might be consulted by missions sent to Rome to explain and obtain a decision upon this knotty point. But John was not in any doubt that De Gray must have the appointment. The monks however wanted their sub-prior Reginald to have it and therefore provisionally and secretly elected him before they sent him off on his mission to Rome. But Reginald was not the soul of discretion. When he reached Rome he announced that he had been elected and asked for papal confirmation. The news percolated back to England. John was exceedingly annoyed (understandably so) and went to Canterbury to demand that the monks should elect John de Gray subject to the assent of the bishops. They promptly did so. But papal confirmation was still required.

RIGHT A scribe at work (Bodleian Roll 167g f95v). Relatively few Englishmen could read and write; they were mainly clerks educated for the Church.

LEFT Innocent III, one of
the greatest of medieval
popes. In the course of his
long struggle with John he
placed England under
an Interdict and
excommunicated the King.

RIGHT The seal of Stephen
Langton, appointed by
Innocent III to be Arch-
bishop of Canterbury
in 1206.

Pope Innocent III was naturally confused by the rival claims
of Prior Reginald and Bishop John de Gray. He therefore sent
for fifteen monks to come from Canterbury and asked that the
bishops of the province and the King should each send proctors
with powers of attorney. Having heard both sides of the case,
he ordered that the first election should be quashed and a new
one held by the delegates from Canterbury. The monks then
divided about equally between the rival candidates. Innocent III
therefore proposed a compromise candidate in Stephen Langton,
an Englishman originally from Lincolnshire, who had taught
in the University of Paris, for whose character and attainments
the Pope had the highest regard and whom he had made a
Cardinal. Langton was then about fifty and had settled in Rome.
In December 1206 the monks from the chapter obediently and
unanimously elected him Archbishop of Canterbury. But John

Choir practice from an illumination in a thirteenth-century manuscript (Bodleian MS Douce 50)

would not accept his election, nominally on the ground that Langton had been living among his enemies and was quite unknown to him. When on 17 July 1207 Innocent III consecrated Langton as Archbishop, John promptly replied by laying hold of the revenues of Canterbury Cathedral and driving the monks into exile. Thus John directly challenged the authority of the Pope, and two determined rulers faced each other in fierce conflict. Reason gave way to anger; yet a compromise was perfectly possible. For the Pope always recognised that episcopal appointments needed the approval of the King, while John fully accepted the right of the chapter to elect and the Pope to confirm.

On 27 August 1207 Innocent III nominated a commission of three bishops – the Bishops of London, Ely and Worcester – instructing them to lay a general sentence of Interdict upon England if John would not give his consent to the appointment of Stephen Langton. An Interdict was a weapon that the Pope had used before, for example, against Philip II of France in 1199. It meant that all the church services in the kingdom must be

suspended except baptism of infants and confession of the dying. Furthermore in November the Pope appealed to the barons as good Roman Catholics to support him in this matter against their king, and he warned them that they could not serve two masters. But the sympathies of the barons were with John who, they thought, was being dictated to by a foreign potentate: 'he had been flouted by a troublesome chapter and an interfering Pope' (Frank Barlow). On 23 March 1208 therefore the Interdict was proclaimed.

John took immediate reprisals. He appointed a commission to seize and sequestrate the entire property of the Church, from the lands of wealthy bishops down to the humble glebes of the parish priests. But the resulting confusion should not be exaggerated. John allowed the clergy sufficient means for their maintenance. It is true that he arranged for the arrest of all the clergy's housekeepers or concubines; many of the English clergy, although supposedly celibate, had mistresses. But they were allowed to have them back on the payment of fines. Moreover the church courts continued to function as usual (though appeals to Rome were prohibited), church building continued and the church festivals were kept. Services were held

A Franciscan friar hearing a nun's confession. The first two orders of friars, the Franciscans and Dominicans, were founded in the early thirteenth century. Their aim was to bring back the ideals of those who had followed Christ in a life of poverty and self-denial.

in the open air, and the Pope allowed conventual churches to celebrate Mass behind closed doors. Later he granted permission for the last communion to be administered to the dying. Neither the baronage nor ordinary people seem to have been unduly upset by the Interdict, while the King was able to improve his finances by using the funds of the Church.

Behind the scenes, as generally happens, negotiations went on between the opposing parties. In October 1209 Stephen Langton, who was a man of blameless life and an English patriot, arrived at Dover on John's invitation, but he was not allowed to meet the King. His brother Simon had earlier been permitted to see the King though nothing came of his visit. A papal legate was also sent over from Rome to treat with John. In November 1209, after Stephen Langton had returned to France, Innocent III excommunicated King John and the bull of excommunication was published in all the churches of northern France. Excommunication was really a more dangerous penalty for John than the Interdict had been, because it undermined loyalty, allowing discontented barons to rebel against him, and because it empowered the King of France to attack him if he wished. But John would not be moved. In 1211 he said that if Stephen Langton ventured into England again he would have him hanged. He was indifferent to the fact that by the end of 1211 there was only one consecrated bishop, Peter des Roches, Bishop of Winchester, left in England.

While it is generally agreed, so far as our knowledge goes, that the Interdict had comparatively little effect on King John or his subjects, it seems clear that in the long run his excommunication made a considerable impression. For when once more in the summer of 1211 John refused the terms offered by the Pope for reconciliation, the legate Pandulf not merely excommunicated the King at Northampton in front of most of the leading barons of England, but absolved the King's subjects from their oaths of allegiance and threatened him with deposition. The news of the papal sentence reinvigorated the unruly Welsh and in the following summer John was obliged to summon the feudal host to Chester to put down a rising. Uneasy rumblings were heard in Ireland too and in August at Nottingham John received messages from Scotland and Wales warning him that some of his barons were plotting against him,

Church Architecture

The end of the twelfth century saw the transition from Romanesque or Norman architecture to Gothic in England. The main features of Norman architecture were the rounded arch and the rounded barrel vault, supported by massive pillars. Gothic architecture was characterised by the pointed arch, which is much more slender and light in form, enabling the builder to produce the soaring cathedrals of the later Middle Ages.

ABOVE The church of St Mary and St David, Kilpeck, an excellent example of late Romanesque architecture. Around the top of the church runs a corbel table with imaginative carved supports.
LEFT Arcading in the Chapter House at Much Wenlock Priory in Shropshire. It clearly demonstrates the transitional period as it consists of Norman rounded arches interlaced to produce Gothic lancets.

RIGHT The nave of Salisbury Cathedral looking westwards. It is 230 feet long.

BELOW Salisbury Cathedral, a magnificent example of Early English architecture. The cathedral shows a perfect uniformity of style, since it was all built between 1220 and 1266, with the exception of the spire.

Two Cistercian
monks conversing.

aiming to murder or depose him. Meanwhile Peter of Wakefield,
a Yorkshire hermit with a gift for prophesying, forecast that the
King would not survive next Ascension Day.

John was sufficiently alarmed to abandon his Welsh campaign
and dismiss his feudal host; and he clapped Peter of Wakefield
into prison at Corfe Castle and later had him put to death. When
it was known that two leading barons, Robert fitz Walter of
Dunmow in Essex and Eustace de Vesci of Alnwick in
Northumberland, had fled the country to join the exiled
bishops, it suggested to John that a good foundation existed for
the rumours of conspiracy. William Marshal, Earl of Pembroke,
who had now made up his quarrel with the King and had since
1210 been serving him nobly in Ireland, advised John to put an
end to his quarrel with the Papacy which had helped to give
rise to such a dangerous internal situation. Innocent III was in
fact preparing to play his trump card by issuing letters of
deposition. These letters, which were given to Cardinal
Stephen Langton at Christmas 1212, called upon King Philip of

ſet tnii v. Adutonū nrm ī noīe d̄.
uoiaʒo te
ecatura
ſatis p de
um u
uum. pa
daun
uctun. p

A priest conducting a service assisted by a server.

France to implement John's deposition. Philip was only too delighted to carry out the Pope's instructions. In the spring of 1213 he summoned his vassals to Rouen, concentrated an army and a fleet at Boulogne, and entered into discussions with his son, Louis, whom he designed to be the new King of England, on what their future relations should be.

But John had already taken action, possibly on William Marshal's advice. In November 1212 he dispatched a mission to Rome to inform Pope Innocent III that he would accept the terms which he had refused in the previous year. The papal legate, Pandulf, who had been engaged in giving encouragement to French plans for the cross-Channel invasion, thereupon ordered that they would be suspended and hurried over to England to discover if the King was in earnest. John was well aware that he could not deceive the Pope, and therefore determined to go the whole hog. What Innocent III had required in 1211 was that John should submit to ecclesiastical discipline for his offences against the Church, that he should receive

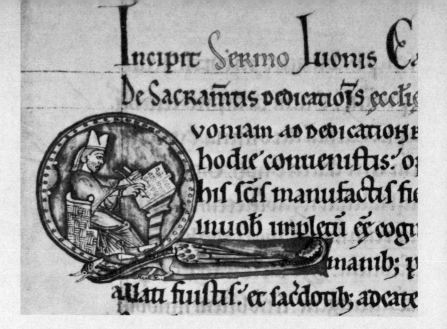

A bishop writing, from an illumination in a twelfth-century manuscript. He is seated in a basket chair.

Stephen Langton as Archbishop of Canterbury, and take back all the exiled bishops, clergy and laity (now including the rebellious Robert fitz Walter and Eustace de Vesci) and that he should pay compensation for all the property that he had stolen from the Church. John went much farther than simply to agree to these terms. When he met Pandulf at Dover on the eve of Ascension Day 1213, he not only promised to be 'faithful to God, to St Peter, to the Church of Rome and to my liege Lord Pope Innocent and his Catholic successors' but he issued a charter, witnessed by John de Gray, Justiciar of Ireland, Geoffrey fitz Peter, the Chief Justiciar of England, and several other leading barons, declaring that of his own free will he acknowledged the Pope as his overlord for the whole kingdoms of England and Ireland. In return for a tribute of 1,000 marks a year John was to be accepted as a liege vassal of the Papacy.

The legate Pandulf immediately returned to France and, to the fury of Philip II, called off the planned invasion of England which had been designed as a Crusade to depose the excommunicated King John. The English King then invited Stephen Langton and the exiled bishops who were in France or elsewhere to come over to England. In July 1213 he met them at Winchester where Langton, after requiring the King to swear a fresh coronation oath, absolved him from excommunication. On 26 September another important papal legate, Cardinal Nicholas de Romanis, Bishop of Tusculum, arrived in England to clear up the final details of the settlement. He was greeted

ribus uite pdicando quos pfenti laudatoria
litiris pfundebant. A[et mo]ra: credicerunt
multi z bapti[z]abant. imitantes simplici-
tate innocentis uite. ac dulcedine doctrine

sus[t]uere. in pace catholica secul bir[?]
nem euangelizandi gentibz p dn̄o le
suscip[?]ur qui sem[?] pascha sacra p
unitati eccē [??]a faciebant. Q[?] cu[?]

enthusiastically and advised the returned bishops to accept
King John's offer of 100,000 marks to pay for the damage he
had done to Church property and revenues during the Interdict.
The bishops did not think highly of this offer and believed
(rightly) that King John had got off far too easily. The Pope
however in due course instructed the English archbishop and
bishops to consent to a down payment of 40,000 marks and on
29 June 1214, to the ringing of bells and the chanting of the
Te Deum in St Paul's Cathedral, the legate lifted the Interdict.
It had lain upon England for over six years.

Thus did King John and Pope Innocent III stand on their
heads. John agreed to the appointment of Cardinal Stephen
Langton as his Archbishop of Canterbury, an appointment
against which he had fought the Papacy and the Church since
1205. Innocent III welcomed John as a foremost son of the
Church, whose rule and that of his son, the future Henry III, he
henceforward backed to the uttermost. But there was an
unusual coda to this medieval symphony. Langton himself did
not approve of John's surrender of his kingdom to the Pope and
thought that the King's conduct required not merely contrition
and monetary reparation but active co-operation in political
and social reforms. The legate Pandulf was soon to report to
Innocent III that Langton was not helpful in the new regime.
In the summer of 1215 Innocent III suspended Langton from his
functions as Archbishop of Canterbury. John must have been
highly amused.

Monks from the Cenobite
Monastery, from a
thirteenth-century
manuscript.

91

King John as Ruler 1199-1213

KING JOHN, it has well been said, stands out from the pages that record the history of his reign. He 'ruled with reasonable industry' (*'satis laboriose'*), wrote one contemporary chronicler. He dominated his barons and directed his ministers. 'No one in the land could resist his will in anything,' wrote another chronicler. 'The King himself seemed alone to be mighty in the land and he neither feared God nor regarded men.' From his father, Henry II, John had inherited both intelligence of a high order and restless energy. He had also inherited from him an effective machinery of government. Though the King's Court, the *Curia Regis*, centred in the royal household, remained the heart of the government and the ultimate tribunal of appeal, administrative continuity was provided by the Chancery, first under Hubert Walter and later under Richard Marsh, Bishop of Durham, where were recorded under the Great Seal the big transactions of the reign, to which future clerks could refer for precedents. Neat copies of dated charters written upon rolls of parchment made from sheepskins simplified administration and warmed the hearts of future historians. The inauguration of the great series of chancery rolls, the charters, patent, *liberate* and close rolls, though they were generally said to have been the work of Hubert Walter (so Professor Sidney Painter observed), may well have been John's own idea.

If Chancery clerks still accompanied the King as he moved up and down the country, the two other main offices of State, the Exchequer and the Treasury 'had gone out of Court', that is to say they were situated in the capital: the Exchequer was established at Westminster and the Treasury in the Tower of London. The Treasury dealt with the collection of money from many sources and with its expenditure. The Exchequer audited the King's accounts. A Michaelmas audit was recorded in the pipe rolls, which consisted of skins of parchment stitched together at the top with writing on both sides that had to be rolled up for safe keeping. The Exchequer, like the Chancery, had a Great Seal to authenticate its documents. But the barons of the Exchequer did not deal only with financial business; they also came to act as a high court of justice. John laid down in 1201 that cases settled before the barons of the Exchequer had equal validity with those settled before the King or his Justiciar. This was the germ of the Court of Common Pleas.

PREVIOUS PAGES A king dispensing justice from *Le Estoire de St Aedward.*

94

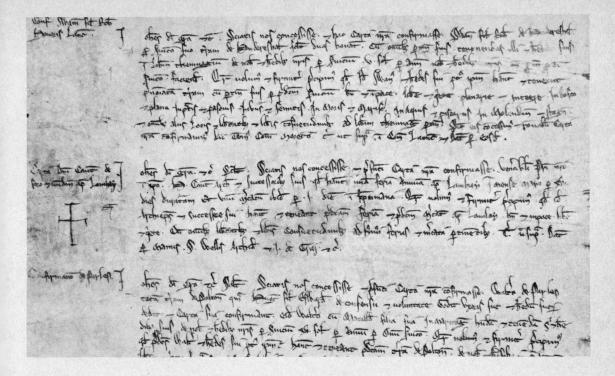

It was sound and relatively sophisticated administrative machinery which had enabled King Henry II to spend much of his life in France and Richard I to absent himself from England for all but a few months of his reign. Thus a restless and energetic king like John was not, so to speak, essential to the day-to-day functioning of government. If he went to war and won glory for himself, as Richard had done, the barons were enchanted to be left alone to attend to their own affairs. It was in fact probably because of the omnipresence of King John in England during so much of his reign – no monarch can ever have been personally more familiar with the highways and byways of his kingdom – that he earned a reputation for being both interfering and arbitrary. As Professor J. C. Holt, the greatest living expert on the reign of King John, has written, 'John's conduct of affairs was not in the main unlawful or contrary to custom. He was making no bid to establish an autocracy.'

The King's penchant for the administration of justice was particularly striking. Having been taught by the great master of jurisprudence, Ranulf de Glanvill, John delighted to show his virtuosity by hearing cases in person as, with his justices and his

Charter roll for the first year of King John's reign, 1199–1200. For three centuries the charter roll was a register for enrolling solemn grants in perpetuity.

An exchequer foil, a piece of wood on which the King's officials recorded money paid to the exchequer.

forty clerks, he moved around his kingdom. He aimed to sell justice cheaply to the poor and deserving and 'he popularised the writ *praecipe* which could be used to transfer a case from the feudal to the royal court' (Frank Barlow). Thus John was a hard-working King who was ably served by a staff which accompanied him on his journeys. Even when John was not himself functioning as a judge, he kept in close touch with the activities of the royal courts of law. John's reputation as a fountain of justice was such that individual subjects felt that they could appeal to him when local courts had failed them. He regarded it as his royal duty to temper the law for the benefit of women and children and the poor. While a court was always available at Westminster to try important cases, John also believed in the value of an itinerant court taking justice to the shires. So John played a valuable part in developing the common law. But his decisions and his zealous manipulation of justice did not always please his wealthier subjects. They particularly disliked the use of the writ *praecipe* and sometimes resented the heavy penalties imposed upon them for mis-demeanours. John understood perfectly well the distinction between the will of the king and the customs of the land and sometimes undoubtedly made use of the former to keep his barons in order. That was why they called him arbitrary.

The taxes and feudal dues collected by John also caused him to be unpopular with his wealthier subjects. For he was certainly no fiscal reformer. The huge debts that he had inherited from his brother and the vast expenses of the wars against Philip Augustus meant that he was in constant need of money and he exploited his rights to the utmost. He levied scutage after scutage. Whereas Henry II had, during the thirty-five years of his reign, levied only eight scutages and Richard had levied only two, John imposed eleven in fifteen years. Moreover, though the traditional sum was one mark or one-and-a-half marks per knight's fee, John levied six scutages at the rate of two marks, one at two-and-a-half marks, and twice attempted to obtain three. (In fairness it must be remembered that the value of money declined in John's reign as compared with that of his father. John had to pay three times as much as his father had done to hire knights.) John also sold offices on a lavish scale, profited from debts contracted to Jews who came under his

96

Instruments of
government in
thirteenth-century
England: charter and
patent rolls in which the
King's grants to his
tenants were recorded.

G

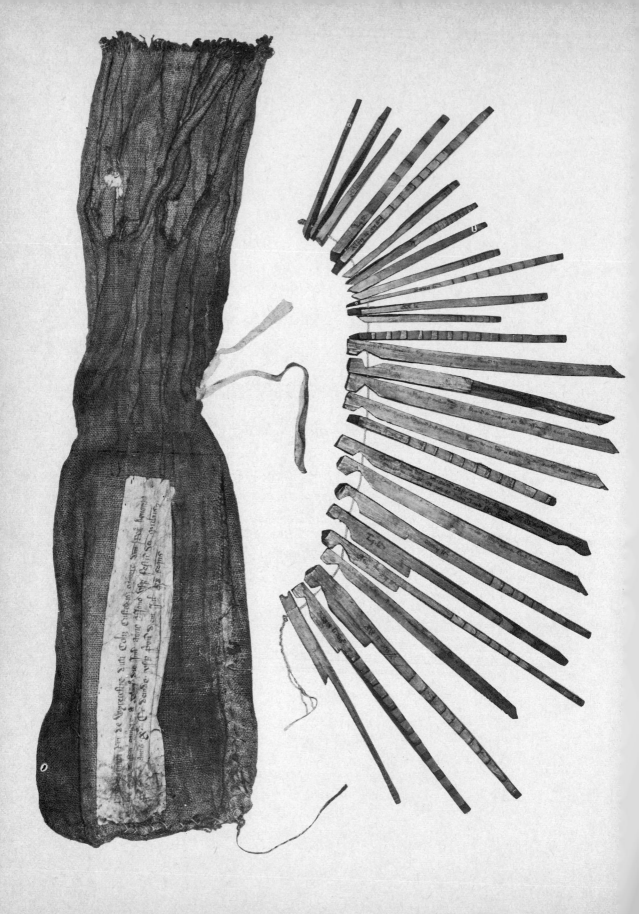

special protection, imposed tallages (or taxes) on the manors and boroughs that lay within the royal demesne, fined or 'amerced' lesser landholders for minor offences and collected all the aids, reliefs and profits of royal wardships to which he was entitled. Moreover he demanded and obtained the payment of special property taxes, disguised under the more agreeable name of 'gracious aids', to meet the costs of his military campaigns; in 1203 he collected a seventh, and in 1207 a thirteenth, of the value of all the movables, chattels and regular revenues of his free subjects. For some four years he introduced customs duties on trade between England, France and Flanders. These set precedents for future kings. Finally in 1212 he instituted an inquiry, hundred by hundred, into the ownership of lands formerly held in chief of the Crown. The barons naturally feared that John was contemplating either increasing the number of knights' fees for which they were responsible or resuming royal lands that had been alienated to them in the past.

John was particularly concerned to preserve the value of money. For that reason he exerted himself to maintain the weight and fineness of the coinage: for the silver penny, the unit of currency, could easily be clipped or debased. Heavy punishments were introduced for false moneyers and on the whole the silver coinage appears to have kept its purity in both England and Ireland. But the main cause of rising costs during most of John's reign was price inflation due to heavy demand. Price inflation was of value to landlords and tenants who had surplus produce to offer for sale, but it was of little or no advantage to the king, who had to buy supplies on a large scale to feed his armies, pay higher rates to his mercenaries and whose own revenues from his lands tended to be fixed over a long period in advance. How to sustain and support mercenary armies was a problem that worried all rulers in the Middle Ages. John was in fact more successful than most since his efficient administration screwed every possible penny out of his feudal rights and he also obtained a windfall by temporarily confiscating the properties of the Church. But confiscation and high taxation by governments are always unwelcome and John's leading subjects nursed a growing sense of grievance which could only be alleviated if he was as uniformly victorious as his brother had been in waging foreign wars.

INCIP PÍATIO S' HIERONIMI ILIBRŪ HESTER
IBRŪ ESTER VARIIS TRANSLATIB:

'The justice of the King', an illustration to the Book of Esther from a twelfth-century manuscript. It demonstrates the contemporary idea of the strong king as the ultimate power in the land.

During the middle years of his reign John was principally occupied in keeping the peace on the frontiers where England met Scotland and Wales, and with affirming his lordship over Ireland. Ireland had not been subjected to England until the reign of Henry II, but long before that William the Conqueror had compelled the King of the Scots (Malcolm III, known as Bighead) to do him homage, while in order to restrain the restless Welsh chieftains the Conqueror had chosen leading Norman barons as 'Marcher Lords' to whom he gave large powers and compact territories in return for their maintaining order on the frontier. Among these lordships were Chester, Shrewsbury, Hereford, Gloucester and later Pembroke. John, as Earl of Gloucester during his brother's reign, was therefore fully aware of the problems on the borders of Wales. He also knew Ireland at first hand from his visit there in 1185; and he learned of the troubles caused to England by the Scottish kings during his peregrinations around northern England. In fact the fortunes of war swung to and fro on the borders of Wales and Scotland and it needed not only the care of the Marcher Lords but the personal backing of a strong king to procure law, order and peace.

The Scottish kings long held the view that their frontier with England should not lie along the River Tweed but that their rule should be extended to cover Northumberland and Cumberland, for they believed, not unreasonably, that the possession of Carlisle and Newcastle upon Tyne was essential to their military security. For a time when Stephen was King of England the Scottish monarchs actually occupied these northern counties, but King Malcolm IV, who was known as the Maiden because of the chastity of his life, surrendered them to the notably less chaste Henry II. Malcolm was succeeded by his brother William the Lion – so called not because he was lion-hearted but because he was thought to be a lion of justice – an ambitious ruler who was determined to assert his independence and regain the lost counties. But he was defeated in battle by Henry II who took him prisoner, sent him to Normandy, obliged him to do homage for Scotland, and forced him to surrender his strongest castles. But the eagerness of Richard I to leave England and go on Crusade gave William the Lion a

An illustration from the Chronicle of Matthew Paris of the story of a knight who pardoned his father's murderer who had taken refuge at the Cross.

chance to regain his authority. By agreeing to pay Richard I 10,000 marks towards the cost of his trip to the Holy Land, William recovered his independence, the English King renouncing his claim to homage; the treaty between them was concluded at Canterbury on 5 December 1189, John attesting as a witness.

As soon as John became king, William the Lion took advantage of the dispute over the succession to attempt to regain the lost counties of Northumberland and Cumberland. He backed Arthur of Brittany, who was his sister's grandson, conspired with John's enemies, and demolished one of the English frontier castles at Tweedmouth. John, who was chiefly concerned with trying to secure his inheritance in France, at first played for time. Then on 22 November 1200 William the Lion did homage to John at Lincoln, but pressed his claims to Northumberland, Cumberland and Westmorland. John refused his assent to these demands and made sure the counties were in the hands of trustworthy royal agents. During the first ten years of John's reign there was constant friction between England and Scotland.

In 1209 the English King determined to settle matters once and for all with the King of the Scots. He mobilised a large army, which even included Llewelyn of Gwynedd, the leading Welsh chieftain, and marched north. John confronted William the Lion at Norham on the Scottish frontier. William was now an old man (he ruled over Scotland for nearly fifty years) and preferred to capitulate rather than to fight. By a treaty concluded on 7 August 1209, William agreed to abandon all his claims, to pay John 15,000 marks and surrender two of his daughters as hostages. He also did homage and in 1212 placed his only son, a boy named Alexander, in John's care, for William was desperately anxious that his son should succeed him peacefully. John repaid his trust, for he later helped to suppress the rebellion of a Scottish pretender from Ireland and in December 1214 Alexander II obtained his father's throne without opposition. In 1221 Alexander was to marry John's eldest daughter, Joan, and thus he became brother-in-law of the then King of England, Henry III.

In 1210 John turned his attention to Ireland. Here personal factors entered into his calculations. John was eager to assert his

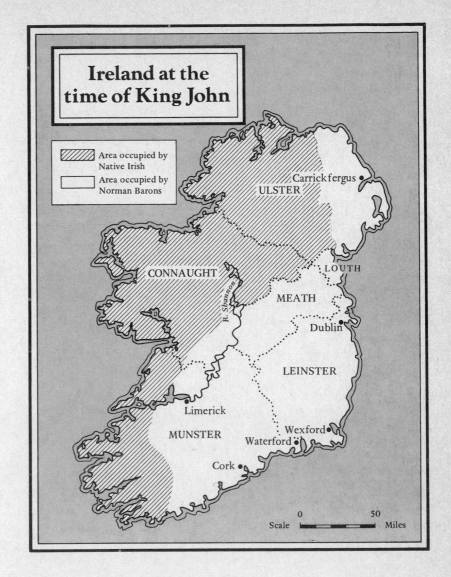

Ireland at the time of King John

Area occupied by Native Irish

Area occupied by Norman Barons

ULSTER

Carrickfergus

CONNAUGHT

LOUTH

MEATH

R. Shannon

Dublin

LEINSTER

Limerick

Wexford

MUNSTER

Waterford

Cork

Scale 0   50 Miles

own authority over the extremely powerful Anglo-Norman barons who were able, from the comparative security of Ireland, to defy him with impunity. Some of these barons, such as William Marshal, Earl of Pembroke and William de Braose, were also Marcher Lords in Wales, but once they got across the Irish Sea they tended to think that they could do much as they liked since they were beyond the King's reach. These Norman barons, who had assisted Henry II in conquering Ireland, occupied vast estates there: William Marshal was Lord of Leinster, William de Braose Lord of Limerick, for which he

Two Irishmen from
Connaught sitting
in a coracle (Bodleian
Roll 187c Fr
Giraldus Cambrensis).

had promised John payment of 5,000 marks, Hugh de Lacy was
Lord of Ulster and his brother Walter de Lacy was Lord of
Meath. The native Irish princes and chieftains had been unable
to resist the Norman barons who drove them north and west
and held down two-thirds of the country with their castles and
garrisons. The only lands owned by the English King himself
were in the 'Pale' round Dublin and Waterford. The King's
Justiciar, Meiler fitz Henry, one of the original Norman
conquerors of Ireland, operated from Dublin, but he was
neither so rich nor so powerful as other Norman barons; he
was actually a vassal of William Marshal, for most of his lands
lay in Leinster. Meiler did not possess the means to do the King's
will in Ireland. Thus John had to go there himself if he wished
to discipline the greater Norman barons.

The cause of John's quarrel with William Marshal, Lord of
Leinster, is clear. He not unnaturally resented the way in which
Marshal accepted Philip II of France as his liege lord for his
properties on the other side of the English Channel and therefore
refused to accompany John on his expedition to Poitou in 1206.
Marshal was an experienced magnate of vast discretion who
wisely decided to keep cool however fierce the provocations
from the King. When Meiler seized possession of the land and
castle of Offaly in Leinster from William Marshal and claimed

to have done so as Justiciar acting under orders from the King, Marshal contented himself with sending a protest to England. After Marshal was summoned to England by the King in the autumn of 1207 and kept by him at the royal Court, John encouraged Meiler to attack William Marshal's lands in Leinster during his enforced absence. But Marshal had taken good care to arrange for the protection of Leinster while he was away, more especially as he had been obliged to leave his wife there as she was pregnant; and Meiler was decisively defeated by William Marshal's knights. Finally John agreed to a compromise. In March 1208 he granted the Earl a new charter for Leinster, which he and his heirs were to hold in fief for the service of a hundred knights, and Marshal also promised the King 300 marks for the restoration of Offaly. William Marshal was then allowed to return to Leinster, King John holding on to two of his sons as hostages and all his castles in England. The unhappy Meiler fitz Henry was removed from office as Irish Justiciar.

John's quarrel with William de Braose was more complicated and more obscure. The De Braoses had come to England with William the Conqueror and had prospered exceedingly. At the beginning of the reign William de Braose stood high in John's favour; John granted him the Gower peninsula in Wales, as

An Irish king standing in a bath surrounded by his subjects, all of them eating mare's flesh (Bodleian Roll 187c Fr8).

'I will not
deliver my sons
to your lord,
King John'

well as giving him Limerick in Ireland in return for a payment of 1,000 marks a year for five years. But in 1207 John broke with him, deprived him of all his offices, and impounded his lands and castles in Wales and the Welsh Marches. The late Dr Austin Lane Poole wrote that 'his sudden downfall in 1207, like so many incidents of John's reign, is unaccountable'. Was it because he had sided with his friend William Marshal against the King? Could it have been because his son Giles, Bishop of Hereford, had approved the Interdict and then fled abroad? Might it have been as John himself insisted, simply because he owed the Exchequer large sums of money which he grossly failed to pay? Or was it because (as the late Sir Maurice Powicke dramatically supposed) William de Braose, who had captured Arthur of Brittany at Mirebeau, knew the dreadful secret of Arthur's death and John decided that this former chosen companion of his 'knew too much to be allowed to live after he and so many others had quarrelled with the King'? According to Roger of Wendover, a chronicler whose account of John's reign is of extremely limited value, when John demanded hostages of William de Braose, his wife, Matilda, defiantly retorted: 'I will not deliver my sons to your lord, King John, for he foully murdered his nephew Arthur, whom he should have cared for honourably.' Though De Braose rebuked his wife, the damage had been done.

The most likely explanation is that John deliberately decided to make a public example of one of the most powerful Norman barons in England, Wales and Ireland, whom he punished as a recalcitrant debtor in accordance with the existing law of the Exchequer. When John asked for hostages, De Braose refused them. When John took hold of three of his castles in Wales as security for his debts William de Braose actually attacked the castles that he had surrendered and tried to win them back. Finally, in the winter of 1208–9, to escape John's wrath over his conduct, William de Braose fled with his wife and two sons to Ireland, where he was met by his friend, William Marshal, and conducted by him to a safe refuge in Meath, whose lord, Walter de Lacy, was William de Braose's son-in-law.

At the end of May 1210 King John assembled a feudal host, together with Flemish knights and mercenaries, at the port of Haverford in Pembrokeshire, resolved, as he announced, finally

Two noble ladies captured and fettered.

to settle the De Braose affair. William de Braose came over to see John at Haverford and offered to settle with him by paying a fine of 40,000 marks. As he was already deeply in debt to the Exchequer, it is hard to know how he intended to raise the money. In any case John would not be appeased; he was convinced that Matilda de Braose was the real head of the family and was determined to punish her and those who were sheltering her in Ireland.

On 20 June 1210 John landed near Waterford where he was joined by John de Gray, the trusted bishop whom he had tried to appoint Archbishop of Canterbury and who had replaced

Trim Castle in County Meath in Ireland, completed in its
present form in the 1190s. It is said to have been the largest military
stronghold that was built in medieval Ireland.

Meiler fitz Henry as Irish Justiciar in 1208. Accompanied,
presumably with reluctance, by William Marshal, John made a
leisurely progress through Leinster to Dublin. John's army had
fastened like locusts on William Marshal's chief seat in Ireland.
Marshal was so fabulously rich that he was able to bear these
depredations with equanimity. Finally at Dublin John charged
Marshal with sheltering his enemy, William de Braose, when
he first fled from Wales to Ireland. Marshal refused to be in-
timidated and asserted that William de Braose was his overlord
(presumably for some of his possessions in western England)
and that therefore it was his feudal duty to protect him. The old
knight, hero of a thousand tournaments, now in his sixty-
seventh year, offered to fight any baron who called him a liar.
John contented himself with demanding four of William
Marshal's knights as hostages and taking possession of one of his
Irish castles. As John already held all William Marshal's castles

in England and two of his sons as hostages, he could be reasonably sure of Marshal's good behaviour.

The other Anglo-Norman barons in Ireland got off less lightly. While John showed favour to the native Irish chieftains, whose submission he graciously accepted, he completely dispossessed Walter de Lacy, the Lord of Meath, and when his brother, Hugh de Lacy, attempted to resist the King in Ulster, John turned his defences in the Mountains of Mourne, outflanking him by personally taking a contingent of picked warriors by sea, and surrounded his stronghold at Carrickfergus. Hugh de Lacy and Matilda de Braose, whom he had taken into his care, fled by ship to Scotland. As soon as Hugh de Lacy had gone, the garrison surrendered.

Thus within two months, without fighting a single battle, John subdued the proud Anglo-Norman barons and established his own authority as Lord of Ireland. It was a very different story from what had happened twenty-five years earlier when as a young and headstrong prince he had been humiliated by the Irish kings and rebuked by his father. For the remainder of John's reign 'Norman Ireland became peaceful, prosperous and loyal' (Frank Barlow). John's justiciars in Ireland extended the royal authority and codified the law. A new stone castle which was built in Dublin symbolised John's triumph.

The De Braoses did not escape John's anger. Matilda and her eldest son were captured in a now submissive Scotland and handed over to the English king who imprisoned them in Windsor Castle. According to most of the monastic chroniclers, they were starved to death, though where or when is uncertain. William de Braose, after vainly trying to ransom his wife, fled to France where he died an exile in September 1211. Stephen Langton conducted his funeral. Yet John by his ruthless treatment of this great feudal lord had not succeeded in terrifying his other barons in England, but rather the contrary. After his return from Ireland he thought it worth while to publish a proclamation giving his version of the story, telling of De Braose's huge debts to the Crown and of his disloyal resistance to the occupation of his castles. Half of the barons who witnessed this document were to be found among the leaders of the rebels against the King in 1215.

Wales proved to be a more intractable problem to John than

Manorbier Castle in Pembrokeshire, one of the border castles, built in the twelfth and thirteenth centuries.

either Scotland or Ireland. Peace there depended on a delicate balance of forces. On the one hand, there were Welsh princes who quarrelled with one another but were equally capable of uniting against the kings of England and their Marcher Lords. Many of the Welshmen, who were fine guerrilla soldiers and devout Christians, nursed the ideal of complete independence. 'The defence of their native land and liberty,' wrote Gerald of Wales, 'is their sole concern: they fight for fatherland and they labour for liberty. ... They deem it ignoble to die in their beds and an honour to fall in the field of battle.' In spite of English penetration into Pembrokeshire and Glamorgan in South Wales, this ideal persisted and Welsh heroes were often to be found at Gwynedd amid the fastnesses of Snowdonia.

The kings of England could not altogether rely for the defence of the frontier on their Marcher Lords who tended to exploit their unique position in order to increase their own wealth and even to defy the monarchy. At the beginning of his reign John tried to maintain the balance of power, first by playing off the Welsh chieftains against one another and secondly by relying on the Marcher Lord Ranulf, Earl of Chester in the north and the Marcher Lords William Marshal and William de Braose, in the south. The most forcible figure in Wales was Llewelyn the Great (Llewelyn ap Iorworth), Prince of Gwynedd, who was the grandson of an earlier Welsh hero known as Owen the Great. In 1201 Llewelyn did homage to John for all his lands in north Wales and in 1204 he married John's illegitimate daughter, Joan. In 1208 he extended his influence by conquering southern Powys in central Wales and in 1209 he showed his loyalty to his overlord and father-in-law by serving with John's army in Scotland.

But in 1210 a break came. The reason was that the balance of power had been upset. The disgrace of William Marshal and William de Braose had left a dangerous gap in the English defences while Llewelyn had become dominant in northern Wales. Flushed with his triumph in Ireland, John decided to impose his authority upon Wales and teach his son-in-law a lesson. The ease with which he had been able to march through South Wales on his way to and from Ireland made him over-confident. So when in May 1211 he gathered an army at Chester and invaded northern Wales he was taken by surprise at the difficulty of the terrain and the skilful guerrilla tactics of Llewelyn's Celtic warriors. John was compelled to withdraw because his army was threatened with starvation.

However he was not easily defeated. In July he reformed his troops at Oswestry, north-west of Shrewsbury, calling up reinforcements and arranging for ample supplies of provisions. He led his army up the Conway River towards Bangor, which was burned to the ground, and Llewelyn was obliged to conclude what he regarded as a shameful peace. John occupied the area known as the Fourt Cantrefs between Snowdonia and Chester and thus pinned down Llewelyn in Caernarvonshire. He also imposed a heavy tribute and took thirty hostages. At the same time, John's favourite mercenary commander, Falkes de Bréauté, whom he had placed in charge of Glamorgan after the flight of William de Braose, occupied northern Carmarthenshire and built a castle at Aberystwyth.

But these humiliations rallied the whole Welsh people behind Llewelyn for it looked to them as if their national identity was to be crushed out of existence. Thus in the summer of 1212 the Welsh rose again and captured two of the King's castles. They were inspired in their ardour by the Pope. John angrily had some of the Welsh hostages hanged and ordered the feudal host to gather at Chester. But, as has been observed, rumours of a plot against his life induced John to abandon his campaign. Llewelyn in fact was saved from disaster by the restlessness of the English barons. He recovered the Four Cantrefs in 1213 and moved nearer to becoming a native Prince of Wales. It was left to John's grandson, King Edward I, to capture the princedom of Wales for the English royal line.

These three campaigns in 1209–11 revealed John's genius as both a commander and a military organiser. The march to the Scottish border, the assault upon Ulster, and the advance from Oswestry to Bangor all showed different facets of his skill in war. He could plan cleverly, act with remarkable speed (just as he had done when he took Mirebeau) and he appreciated how to outflank his enemies by exploiting the use of rivers and the sea. Now he was to be faced with further campaigns. First he attempted to regain his ancestral lands in France; then he was confronted with a rebellion in England which aimed to topple him from his throne.

'They fight for fatherland and they labour for liberty'

nonaf nouembuf capta est damieta siue d
one absq̃ tumultu 7 uiolentia expliatione
filio dei uictoria ascribatur. Et cum caperet
tituf inculif regif babilonif. n̄ fuit ausus more s
anof aggredi. s; confusus anfugienf ꝺ̃a castra
sic. Expoꝛtaq; dux militerf q̃i damietam ingꝛ

Turrif damiate

5
The Struggle in France
1213-14

apta igitur dainieta . missicione castri dinpicos.
sunt exploratores ad iuxi ville in festo sci cle
mentis in nauiculis p paruum flumen quod tap
nis appellatur. ut de castellulis 7 villis uictuali
a quererent 7 sic locorum diligentia explorarent.
bium aut appropinquissent ad castrum quoddam de

Ciuitas
Damie

I N THE SPRING OF 1213 King John of England and King
Philip II of France were getting ready to make war on each
other. Indeed ever since the signature of the truce between
them in October 1206 John's whole policy had been directed
towards revenge. His assertion of his authority over the Irish,
the Scots and the Welsh, the strong line that he took with his
most powerful barons, and his resolution to obey the Pope were
all directed to securing his base in England before he set sail
once again for France. Philip II, as has already been noticed,
had been planning to conquer England under the guise of a
holy crusade against an excommunicated King, but had been
frustrated when John opened negotiations for conciliation with
the Papacy. Nevertheless Philip Augustus did not give up his
aggressive intentions and on 22 May 1213 he launched an
assault upon Flanders in preparation for a cross-channel attack
on England.

Both sides had laid diplomatic as well as military foundations
for the war. Philip II had concluded a treaty with Frederick of
Hohenstaufen, King of Sicily, who called himself the Emperor
Frederick II and was contending with Otto, Duke of Brunswick
who called himself the Emperor Otto IV (he had been deposed
by Innocent III in Frederick's favour in 1210) for the succession
to the throne of the Emperor Henry VI. John negotiated with
Otto IV, who was his nephew, for an alliance. Otto was only
too eager to overthrow Philip II who had committed himself
to his rival. Philip Augustus wanted to convert Flanders into a
base for his assault on England and quarrelled with Count
Renaud of Boulogne and Count Ferrand of Flanders when they
refused to assent to his wishes. Philip's army overran Flanders
while his navy and military transports were mobilised near the
Flemish coast.

Since 1212 King John had set about reconstituting the alliance
which Richard I had found so useful in checking the designs of
the French King. In May 1212 the Count of Boulogne had come
to England and concluded a treaty of alliance with John at
Lambeth. In March of the following year the Count of Holland
did homage to John at London in the presence of the Count of
Boulogne and the Count Palatine of the Rhine. Two months
later John received an appeal for help from the Count of
Flanders who was being fiercely attacked by Philip II's army.

PREVIOUS PAGES Battle
scenes from the Chronicle
of Matthew Paris. On the
right soldiers are rushing
up scaling-ladders into
a castle. On the left
soldiers are attacking a
castle by water, using
crossbows, a flail and
slings with stones.

OPPOSITE Frederick II,
King of Sicily and
Jerusalem and Emperor
of Germany.

John thereupon summoned a conference and the decision was taken in favour of an immediate naval attack upon Flanders. Apart from his diplomatic alliances, all the necessary arrangements for war had been made by John. The King had, by various devices, acquired a substantial war chest which was transported to the south of England. Thus he was able to pay for the services of a fleet of five hundred warships which were assembled at Portsmouth under the command of William, Earl of Salisbury. These warships had been trained for their task by engaging in raids upon the French coast and attacks on the shipping in the Seine. John also gathered his land forces at Canterbury and Dover. The fleet sailed on 28 May 1213 with the Counts of Boulogne and Holland and a large number of knights and mercenaries on board.

When the English fleet reached the coast of Flanders on 30 May it entered the estuary of the River Zwyn and reconnaissance revealed that hundreds of French vessels, many of them loaded with stores and supplies, were riding at anchor or beached on the shore of the harbour of Damme, which was the port for Bruges. Moreover it was discovered that only sailors were on guard, the French army then being employed on the siege of Ghent. Salisbury ordered an immediate attack upon the French ships and he also disembarked knights at Damme

OPPOSITE The Emperor Otto IV, son of Henry the Lion, Duke of Saxony and King John's sister, Matilda. Otto was elected emperor in 1208, but two years later he was deposed in favour of Frederick II.

BELOW A sea battle from the Chronicle of Matthew Paris. The boat has been grappled by an anchor and the enemy's ship boarded.

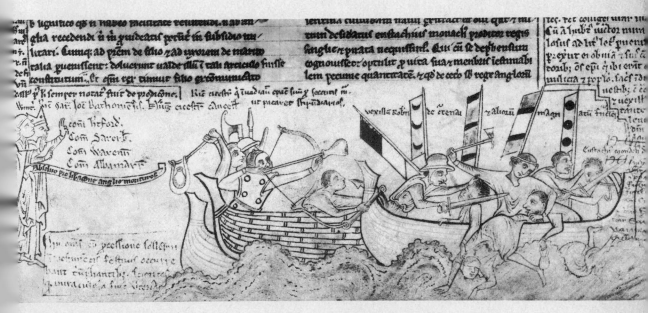

with a view to their supporting the Count of Flanders, who arrived there to conclude an alliance with the English. However, when the main French army returned from Ghent the English knights decided that discretion was the better part of valour and hastily re-embarked. Nevertheless it was a notable victory, for not only had the French invasion fleet been demolished but huge booty had been captured.

Since his arrival in England Cardinal Stephen Langton, who was nothing if not patriotic, had been making himself useful to King John in diplomatic affairs as his predecessor, Hubert Walter, had done. In June he had concluded a truce with the Welsh which was later prolonged. John, having been absolved by Langton from excommunication, was able to devote himself to the arrangements for the next year's campaign. In July he sent an embassy to Germany to negotiate details of an alliance with Otto IV. He decided that he himself would go to Poitou early in the following year. His diplomatic programme having been completed and with the great naval victory of Damme

A knight on horseback, an illumination from a psalter dating from 1200.

behind him, John's only concern was to ensure that his English barons and knights should remain loyal during his absence abroad.

About his barons' loyalty John was by no means satisfied. The northern barons, headed by his old enemy Eustace de Vesci, were extremely recalcitrant. When he invited them to follow him to Poitou or to pay scutage they 'with one mind and determination' (according to the contemporary chronicler Ralph of Coggeshall) 'refused, asserting that according to the tenure of their lands, they were not bound to him in this; besides they were already too much worn out and impoverished by expeditions within the realm'. John answered that they were obliged to obey him by feudal custom and there seems to have been no real justification for their plea for exemption from service overseas. It has been described as 'a compound of bravado and chicanery' (J. C. Holt).

John was extremely angry, and in August 1213 marched north with the intention of punishing these defiant barons. Stephen Langton, who had been engaged in trying to reconcile the King with his leading barons, remonstrated with John, saying that he had no right to wreak his wrath on the northerners without a legal sentence of his Court. John told Stephen Langton that it was none of his business, and Langton had to use threats of excommunication before the King cooled down. He allowed himself to be reconciled to the northerners on 1 November at Wallingford and made some concessions; he also came to terms with his bishops on the indemnity that was to be paid them for the damage done to their property during the Interdict. Early in November he not only summoned his tenants-in-chief to meet him at Oxford but also instructed the sheriffs to select four discreet knights from each shire 'to speak with us concerning the affairs of our realm'. Whether they actually came to meet the King and if so, what they discussed, is not known. But it is possible that King John contemplated using the knights to counterbalance the barons. It would be going rather far to take this episode as a firm precedent for the summoning of knights of the shires to Parliaments as was done in his son's reign.

It is not known what John said to his barons at Oxford. All that can be said is that the relationship between John and his

'To speak with us concerning the affairs of our realm'

123

leading subjects appears to have become extremely delicate during the autumn and winter of 1213. The barons were understandably weary of the burdens that had been placed upon them during the frontier wars and over the money that had been exacted from them in various ways to pay for the King's hired mercenaries. The protests of the northerners were symptomatic of the state of unrest and so were Stephen Langton's efforts to reconcile the King with his barons. There is a story deriving from one of the chroniclers, which may or may not be true, that at this time Archbishop Langton drew the attention of the barons to the coronation charter of King Henry I as pointing a way in which they could establish their rights in relation to the King. Also, a document discovered in the French archives (rather misleadingly called 'the Unknown Charter of Liberties'), which possibly belongs to this period,

Merton College, Oxford, founded by William de Merton in the thirteenth century. It was the earliest college foundation at Oxford. By King John's reign, Oxford was already known as a centre of learning.

appears to have been an outline of a constitutional settlement discussed between the King and his barons. One of the proposals was that the King should concede that his barons were not required to serve in an army outside England except in Normandy or Brittany; another was that scutage should never exceed one silver mark per knight's fee. If more scutage were needed, it should not be levied except with the advice and consent of the barons of the realm.

The situation in England was therefore unsettled when in February 1214 King John started out on his greatest campaign against Philip II of France. Before he left his kingdom he informed the Archbishop of Canterbury and other bishops of his plans. Evidently he relied chiefly on the clergy to maintain order at home while he was away; for he stated that he placed the country 'in the custody and protection of God and the Holy Roman Church and the Lord Pope and the Lord Nicholas Bishop of Tusculum and Legate of the Holy See'. The Justiciar, Geoffrey fitz Peter, had died in the previous October, but it was not until 1 February, on the eve of his departure, that John appointed as his successor Peter des Roches, Bishop of Winchester. Des Roches was a Poitevin who had endeared himself to the King by staying in England throughout the period of the Interdict. He was not popular either with the other bishops or with the lay baronage; but he was an extremely able and efficient statesman entirely loyal to John. He was instructed to co-operate with the Legate and Archbishop Langton.

On 2 February 1214 John embarked at Portsmouth with his Queen, his second son, Richard, and his niece Eleanor of Brittany (sister to the dead Arthur) and a vast quantity of treasure. Few earls accompanied him; old William the Marshal still refused to fight in person against his French overlord, but sent his knights. The majority of the King's troops were lesser knights and mercenaries. After spending a few days at Yarmouth in the Isle of Wight on account of bad weather, John arrived at La Rochelle in Poitou on 15 February. This port was friendly to England with which it did much business. A number of Poitevin barons came to La Rochelle and swore allegiance to the English King. Meanwhile William Longsword, Earl of Salisbury, also set out by sea with English and Flemish mercenaries and plenty of money to lay out in subsidies in order to join John's new allies

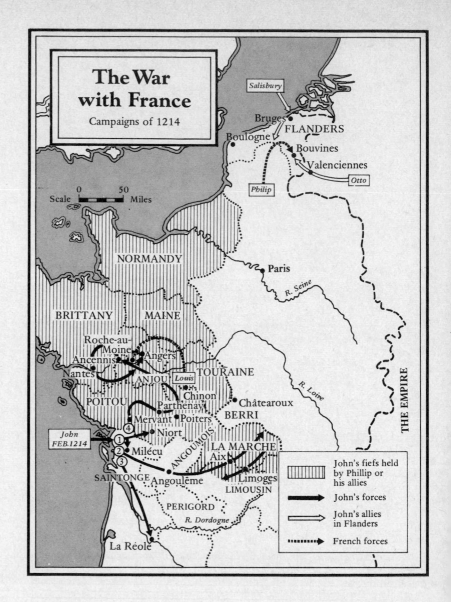

The War
with France
Campaigns of 1214

Scale 0 50 Miles

Salisbury
Bruges
Boulogne
FLANDERS
Bouvines
Valenciennes
Otto
Philip

NORMANDY

Paris

R. Seine

BRITTANY   MAINE

Roche-au-
Moine   Angers
Ancennis
Nantes   ANJOU   *Louis*   TOURAINE   *R. Loire*   THE EMPIRE
Chinon
POITOU   Parthenay   Châtearoux
Mervant   Poiters   BERRI
④   Niort
John   ①   ANGOUMOIS   LA MARCHE
FEB.1214   ②   Milécu   Aix
③
SAINTONGE   Angoulême   Limoges
LIMOUSIN

PERIGORD
R. Dordogne

La Réole

John's fiefs held by Phillip or his allies
John's forces
John's allies in Flanders
French forces

in Flanders. John's strategic plan was that the allied forces in Flanders should hammer the French army on to the anvil of his troops in Poitou.

On 20 February John left La Rochelle and marched to relieve the important neighbouring fortress of Niort, which had long held out against Philip II, and then on towards Poitou as if to show his colours there. On 6 March he returned to La Rochelle to learn that the nearby castle of Milécu, from which one of the Poitevin barons had been defying him, had been quickly

126

reduced. A week later the King was at Angoulême, which had been his wife's birthplace. As he had discovered in 1204, in order to secure his communications through Aquitaine it was essential to command the counties of Angoulême, La Marche and the Limousin. In March he carried out a reconnaissance in this area and evidently concluded a truce with the local baronage and then continued north-west to Berri where he spent Easter. There he received the homage of the Count of Périgord, which lies south of the Limousin. In April John turned south and advanced deep into Gascony, but by 8 May he was over 200 miles to the north in the home of his ancestors, Anjou.

John's intentions in carrying out these somewhat complicated military manœuvres were threefold: first he wanted to reconnoitre the strength of his resources in Aquitaine and Anjou; secondly, he was anxious to impress his presence upon the various local counts and barons; thirdly, he wanted to baffle Philip II, who had left Flanders and was hovering with an army on the borders of Poitou. Philip now determined to give up watching John's swift peregrinations and return to protect his position in Flanders. This enabled John to undertake a major operation aimed at crushing his former enemies, the Lusignans, in Lower Poitou.

There were three Lusignans, Hugh IX, Count of La Marche, Ralph, Count of Eu, and their uncle Geoffrey, a former Crusader much admired by Richard I. John decided to force them to declare themselves on his side. The firmest resisters were Geoffrey and his two sons. John reported back to England his success in achieving his aims:

> You should know [he wrote] that when the truce was at an end which we had granted to the counts of La Marche and Eu, and as we did not find them ready to make peace with us, on the Friday before Pentecost [16 May] we marched with our army to Geoffrey's castle of Miervant; and although many believed it was impregnable to an assault, yet on Whitsun Eve [17 May] we laid siege to another of Geoffrey's castles, called Vouvant, in which he was himself with two of his sons; and when, after a continual battering with our siege weapons for three days its fall was imminent, the Count of La Marche came up and induced Geoffrey to surrender with his two sons, his castle and all that was in it.

On 25 May at Parthenay, west of Poiters, all the Lusignans did

homage and fealty to John, who arranged that his eldest
daughter by Isabelle of Angoulême, who was named Joan (like
her illegitimate half-sister), should be betrothed to Hugh IX's
son, who was also named Hugh. The large number of Poitevin
barons who witnessed the marriage contract was in itself a
proof of John's triumph in central Aquitaine; so was a last-
minute move by Philip Augustus who, having failed to interfere
with John's military progress, now proposed that little Joan
(who was four years old) should marry his own son, Louis. John
was too wily to accept that proposal. After reporting it to his
home government, he added: 'And now by God's grace there
is given us the opportunity to carry out our attack upon our
chief enemy, the King of France, beyond the limits of Poitou.'

John at once resumed his rapid marches. From Parthenay he
turned towards Poitiers and then farther east into Berri. From
Berri he moved down the Loire as if to threaten the city of
Angers from the west and south. But instead of besieging
Angers he went on farther west and on 13 June attacked the
seaport of Nantes at the mouth of the Loire which was occupied
by a French garrison. The port was surprised and quickly taken.
Among the prisoners was a cousin of the French King. Whether
John had the idea of using Nantes as his base instead of La
Rochelle is not known. Nor is it known whether it was the
rapid conquest of Nantes which induced the city of Angers to
open its gates to King John as it did on 18 June; at any rate he
'was once more in the original capital of his forefathers' (Kate
Norgate).

But John then met with a setback. William des Roches, who
had deserted John in 1202 and whom Philip II had appointed
seneschal of Anjou, had built a formidable new castle at
Roche-au-Moine on the Loire, west of Angers. It has been
described as John's 'last hindrance to an advance towards Paris'
(Frank Barlow). Louis, whom Philip II had left with eight
hundred knights to contain John when he himself returned to
Flanders, decided to advance from Chinon in Touraine, where
he was posted, and try to raise the siege of Roche-au-Moine.
The garrison was just about to surrender when the French
King's son arrived. John got ready for a battle which he felt
confident of winning. But the Poitevin barons, who made up
an important part of John's siege army, thereupon announced

N lan de lincarnation. ch.
cc. ou mois de may fu la
pais refournee entre le roy
phc. et le roy jehan dengle
terre. entre vernon et lille dandeli. Si
est plainement contenu es instrumens
autentiques que il firent seeller de leur

ABOVE City walls and a
gateway from a
twelfth-century
manuscript. There was a
steady growth of towns
during the twelfth and
thirteenth centuries, at
first usually founded as
markets under the
patronage of a great lord;
the citizens gradually won
their privileges
which they insisted
upon maintaining.

OPPOSITE The castle of
Angers in Anjou, a vital
fortress which John
recaptured during the
campaign of 1214.

that they were not prepared to fight in the open field. At least,
such is one story, although perhaps they did not want to offend
Philip II by attacking his son. In any case, conscious of treason
in his ranks, John in anger and disappointment allowed Louis
to relieve the castle; he himself withdrew southward across
the Loire on 2 July and a week later was back in his base of La
Rochelle. From there, although he put an optimistic gloss on
events, John wrote to England seeking reinforcements,
begging the barons and knights who had not come with him
to France now to join him.

While John remained immobile in La Rochelle, a conclusive
battle was being fought in Flanders. The Emperor Otto IV, as
he called himself, after lingering at his daughter's wedding in
Aachen, arrived at Valenciennes on 20 July where he joined the
Earl of Salisbury and the Counts of Boulogne, Flanders and
Holland. Philip with his army pressed on to Tournai, but when

ABOVE Cooking scene from a
thirteenth-century manuscript. An
iron cooking pot with an adjustable
pot crane is being used to cook the
meat. On the left a man is
killing a sheep.
LEFT Noble family dining. In front
of the table a servant is slicing bread
on bended knee.

he realised that the allies at Valenciennes were stationed between him and Paris he resolved to retire towards Lille. His route led across the River Marque at the bridge of Bouvines. Philip had the bridge widened and his infantry, baggage and part of his cavalry were across the river when the allies caught up with them on Sunday 27 July after having vainly launched an attack on the French rear guard. Count Reginald of Boulogne was of the opinion that it would be wrong to fight on the Sabbath Day and the Emperor Otto agreed, saying that he had never won a battle on a Sunday, but they were persuaded that their opportunity had come against an enemy who had been surprised and might be disorganised.

The allied army fought in three divisions; on the left were the Count of Flanders and his Flemish knights and infantry; in the centre the Emperor Otto had a mixed force with a front row consisting of pikemen; and on the right the Earl of Salisbury and the Count of Boulogne commanded the forces largely hired and subsidised by King John. The French King brought back his men who had crossed the river and drew his army up on low rolling ground diagonally backing on the east side of the river along a 1,000-yard front which was then extended. The allies were ranged along a 2,000-yard front and the plan appears to have been to assault the French centre, commanded by Philip Augustus himself under a banner of lilies, and then overwhelm it by a converging movement from the two wings. In fact the French on the right opened the battle by charging the Flemings.

It has been estimated that the allied army consisted of some forty thousand men including fifteen hundred knights, and that the French had a slightly smaller force but were stronger in heavy and light cavalry, though weaker in infantry. The battle was fought on a scorching Sunday afternoon in a haze that made it difficult for the contending soldiers to see one another. No real control could be exercised and the fighting soon degenerated into a confused mêlée or huge tournament. The French King was at one stage unhorsed and nearly killed, while the Emperor Otto had three horses killed under him. Possibly the most significant contest took place on the French left and allied right. Here John's mercenaries put up a poor resistance to the mounted French knights. The Bishop of Beauvais, veteran of many a contest, armed with only a club, knocked the

Earl of Salisbury off his horse and took him prisoner. Though the Count of Boulogne fought on until he too was taken prisoner, seven hundred Brabançons, who were under his command and refused to retreat, were slaughtered to a man. The allied centre was also beaten back by French cavalry and when Otto himself rode off the field the Germans and Hollanders lost heart. Only the allied left got off relatively lightly. The Earl of Salisbury, the Count of Boulogne and the Count of Flanders, who had been taken prisoners, were carried in triumph to Paris, where the students of the university celebrated the victory for seven days with 'feasting, leaping and dancing, and singing'. The Earl of Salisbury was finally exchanged for the French King's cousin who had been captured by John at Nantes.

When John learned the news of the disaster at Bouvines, he is reported to have exclaimed – because the Interdict had been lifted from England a month before – 'Since I became reconciled to God and submitted myself and my kingdom to the Church, nothing has gone well with me.' But that must have been just one of those stories. More likely John must have contrasted his own successful campaigning in Aquitaine with the terrible failure in Flanders. John lingered in Poitou for another three months, but all he could do was to come to terms with the French King.

Upon the intervention of a papal legate a nine-day truce was agreed on 30 August while the two sides carried on further negotiations. John had returned to Parthenay while Philip was at Loudon in Anjou so that the two monarchs were only 17 miles apart. The Pope was anxious that the two rulers should stop fighting one another and go off together on a Crusade. The legate acted as mediator in the final conferences. According to a French chronicler, 'the high-souled King Philip ... with his wonted benignity granted a truce'. Another source suggests that King John paid 60,000 marks for a five-year truce, concluded on 18 September, but not taking effect until Easter 1215. The conditions of the truce were that each side should retain their prisoners, that Philip's supremacy in Flanders should be recognised, and that Philip and his adherents should keep all the territory held from the time the truce came into effect. They might continue, if they wished, to support the rival Emperors.

OPPOSITE Battle scene from a twelfth-century psalter.

tota ciuitas parisiaca ticuz z latini cantibz z plau
sibz classicis z laudibz diez z nocte sestiue sericiis z uar
riis ornata pannis sollemit gratulabat. facta z aute
h belli ogressio mense iulio xvi. kl. augusti . -i .

Rex fracoz philippus

Philip Augustus is
unhorsed during the battle
of Bouvines, fought on
27 July 1214 in Flanders.
The battle resulted
in a decisive victory
for the French.

In fact John's nephew Otto died childless in 1218 and Philip's
ally Frederick II, known as 'the Wonder of the World',
succeeded him and became the most brilliant and versatile of
medieval emperors, though he was politically a failure.

John, after wandering about Poitou for a time, returned to
England on 13 October. He found the kingdom peaceful upon
the surface, but beneath it the barons were seething. They hated
the new Justiciar; they resented the levying of a special 'aid' to
pay for the costs involved in the lifting of the Interdict; and their
tempers were not in the least improved when John demanded
that a scutage of three marks for each knight's fee should be
paid by those tenants-in-chief who had refused to accompany
him to Poitou. John was able to soothe the bishops by giving

136

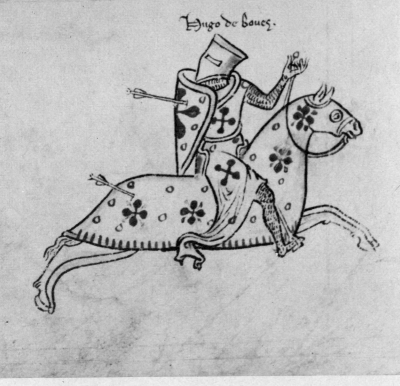

them compensation for the losses they had suffered during the
Interdict, but the ordinary clergy got little or no satisfaction.
On the other hand, the cathedral chapters were conceded the
right freely to elect their bishops.

On the whole, therefore, because of the position he had
assumed as feudatory of the Pope, John had the leaders of the
Church upon his side, but the lay baronage was deeply antag-
onised by the exceptional financial burdens to which it had been
compelled to agree, because of John's unavailing wars to regain
'the Angevin empire' and because of his subservience to the
Papacy. The road from Bouvines to Runnymede, where
Magna Carta was to be sealed, was (in the words of Professor
Holt) 'direct, short and unavoidable'.

6
The Character of King John 1167-1216

IN THIS STUDY OF KING JOHN up to the eve of the great rebellion launched against him in England during the last two years of his life, he has been pictured as an energetic administrator, a first-class general, a clever diplomatist and a ruler who developed the institutions of English law and government. He was also especially wise in his choice of ministers: Hubert Walter, Geoffrey fitz Peter, John de Gray, Peter des Roches, William the Marshal and Hubert de Burgh were all men of outstanding quality. Yet for some seven hundred years British historians wrote of him not merely as a bad man and a bad king but even as a monster, a tyrant and an oppressor. How did this come about? It is partly because most of the medieval chroniclers who first wrote about John's life, being monks, were under the impress of the papal Interdict which brought suffering to the Church in England for nearly half of John's reign. It is only in comparatively recent times, since the administrative records have been combed by expert medievalists, that a more balanced view has emerged.

Matthew Paris, a brilliant chronicler whose *Historia Anglorum* was begun in 1250, thirty-four years after John's death, asserted that 'foul as it is, hell itself is defiled by the fouler presence of John'. Paris worked in the abbey of St Albans and derived his lively version of John's character largely from his predecessor as chronicler there, Roger of Wendover, who wrote his *Flowers of History* also well after John was dead. It has been said by a distinguished twentieth-century historian (V. H. Galbraith) that Paris's portrait of King John is 'a creation of literature as fictitious as Shakespeare's Falstaff'. But Paris merely embroidered upon the writings of Roger of Wendover, whose sinister picture of the King, compounded largely out of prejudice and travellers' tales, created a legend which was accepted for hundreds of years. Indeed Paris produced little more than the caricature which prevailed among the clergy of the time.

None of the chroniclers knew John personally of course and most of them wrote either before he had established himself as a capable monarch or after his death. William of Newburgh observed that John was 'nature's enemy' (*hosti naturae Johanni*), which has been interpreted (wrongly) to mean that he was 'a monster'. The chronicler was in fact writing in about the year

1194, five years before John became King, and all he meant was
that John had been unbrotherly. Gerald of Wales, who did have
some first-hand knowledge of John as a young prince, wrote
of him when he was nineteen:

> Caught in the toils and snared by the temptations of unstable
> and dissolute youth, he was as wax to receive impressions of evil,

142

but hardened against those who would have warned him of its danger; compliant to the fancy of the moment; more given to luxurious ease than to warlike exercises, to enjoyment than to endurance, to vanity than to virtue.

William of Newburgh also noted that John was 'a very foolish youth', and another chronicler observed that he was 'a feckless young man who takes things easily'. All this is the sort of thing which is said every day about teenagers by those who are unaware of the generation gap. Most of the chroniclers who wrote on John when he was a young prince or at the beginning of his reign thought that he had faults. But it was not until he fell foul of the Pope that the sinister portrait emerged.

Bishop Stubbs, a great historian who wrote during the reign of Queen Victoria and himself edited some of the administrative records of John's reign, but nevertheless appears to have placed undue reliance on Roger of Wendover, thought John was 'a worse man than many who have done more harm'. J. R. Green, another brilliant and popular Victorian historian, was prepared to admit that John was 'no weak and indolent voluptuary but the ablest and most ruthless of the Angevins'. Yet he also censured John with true Victorian moral disapprobation as cruel, lascivious and superstitious. Kate Norgate, John's first outstanding modern biographer, writing in 1902, though quoting J. R. Green, stressed John's extortion, oppression and tyranny and, above all, his 'superhuman wickedness'.

These gobbets of moral disapproval continued to be purveyed right up to modern times. Sir Maurice Powicke, writing in the sixth volume of the *Cambridge Medieval History* in 1929 emphasised John's 'treacherous nature'; he also observed that John's 'reason was always at the mercy of his passions', despite the fact that the philosopher David Hume thought that reason should be the servant and not the master of the passions. Powicke concluded that John was 'a thoroughly bad man'. Charles Petit-Dutaillis, a French historian who specialised in early English history, appears to have been the first to apply modern psychological terms to John: he dubbed him a manic-depressive. Professor H. G. Richardson, writing in 1945, soberly observed: 'As for John, his reputation in every field of conduct is beyond redemption, though it is possible that his character may have been unnecessarily blackened by scandalous tongue

'Caught in the toils ... of unstable and dissolute youth'

Neustria Johis huit indefensa sub annis

Quuq: deliquit : gallis possessa reliquit

Johannes rex genuit videlicet.

and pious pen.' Finally Sir Arthur Bryant, in one of his recent colourful books, described John as an 'erratic and moody tyrant' who inherited much of his father's genius but none of his creative capacity, and concluded that he was 'a diabolical maniac' who alienated everyone in turn.

Some modern historians have followed the opinion expressed by J. R. Green that John was an exceptionally able king but a bad man. Professor Sidney Painter, an American historian, in a biography of John published in 1949, considered that he was in most respects an excellent king, but cruel, licentious and deceitful. John T. Appleby, another American author, who published a biography of John in 1959, believed that he was 'an energetic, hard-working and industrious king' but a glutton and a lecher, a faithless husband, a treacherous lord and a godless man; for good measure he added that John was 'a bungling military strategist'. Professor Frank Barlow, who is less inclined to measure men long dead by Victorian ethical standards, observes more mildly that John failed perhaps because he was 'under-endowed with popular virtues' and insists that he was no more of a tyrant than his predecessors. In 1961 Professor W. L. Warren, who wrote the best recent biography of King John, concluded that although John possessed 'the mental abilities of a great king, he had the inclinations of a petty tyrant and was inadequate for the tasks he had to face'. Finally the late Lady Stenton, in her best-selling book on the early Middle Ages, wrote the John had 'a lively mind and a keen intelligence' and was 'no tyrant' but was 'unlucky'. She might perhaps be harking back to one of the more reliable of the chroniclers, the annalist of Barnwell near Cambridge, who wrote ten years after John's death, that he 'was certainly a great prince but hardly a happy one'.

What then is one to think of John's character when so many often contradictory judgments have been passed upon it?

Obviously he inherited a double dose of energy from his father and mother. His father, Henry II, had piled an immense amount of political achievement into his lifetime, though he was no great soldier. Queen Eleanor of Aquitaine was also a dynamo; having borne many children, she fought indomitably on behalf of her favourite son, Richard, almost until she died. John has often been contrasted to his disadvantage with Richard

OPPOSITE King John stag-hunting, from an early fourteenth-century manuscript. Hunting was one of the chief relaxations of kings.

the Lionheart, probably because Richard commanded glamour as a Crusader in the Holy Land, whereas John, until he did homage to the Pope, was an excommunicate son of the Church. This difference reflected itself in the attitude of the monastic chroniclers. But John was just as intelligent as his brother and, like him, did not suffer fools gladly. He was almost as good a soldier if more unlucky; but, after all, what did Richard achieve except to frighten men with an inflated reputation? Richard, like John, has been described as 'a graceless boor'. None of the Angevins in fact were really attractive characters. John was no more cruel, ruthless or 'lascivious' than his elder brother (indeed by Victorian standards of sexual morality Richard was more 'lascivious'); but he might reasonably have felt a grudge against his brother's memory in that he originally denied John's claim to succeed him and apparently only granted it on his death-bed.

Though John clearly inherited characteristics from his parents, including his father's terrible temper (Henry is said to have once chewed a mat in anger), he could not have been deeply influenced by them. Thrust into semi-barbaric Ireland by his father when he was only nineteen – it must have been like a non-swimmer being tipped into a pool – it was hardly surprising that he made mistakes. His brothers induced him to rebel rather

foolishly against his father and it was not until he served with Richard I in France that he had the opportunity of mastering the problems of waging war. John's mother, who loved her son Richard most (perhaps that is why he was homosexual) actually fought against John when Richard was away on Crusade.

John has been described as small, dark and ugly. No contemporary portrait of him exists, though the effigy of him in Worcester Cathedral, made some twenty years after his death, gives an idea of what he looked like. He was 5 foot 5 inches tall and reasonably well-built. His father and two of his elder brothers were considerably taller, a fact that might have given him an inferiority complex. If it is true, as has been said, that he was habitually discourteous, that may have been because he was a proud little man asserting himself.

John liked his comforts, including his baths and his dressing gown. His baths cost him various prices ranging from a penny to five-pence halfpenny each and he is known to have enjoyed them pretty frequently. John was particularly fond of jewellery, including the famous collection he was to lose in the Wellstream estuary, a loss which grieved him deeply. It included a clasp ornamented with emeralds and rubies, given him by the Bishop of Norwich, four rings of emerald, sapphire, garnets and topaz, presented to him by Pope Innocent III, 143 cups of white silver, a wand of gold with a cross given him by the Knights Hospitaller and the regalia which his grandmother Matilda wore when she was crowned Empress. John also spent much time hunting, which, according to Gerald of Wales, was 'a pastime in which he took great and frequent delight': he even hunted on Holy Days. Finally, he liked his food and wine, though whether he was a 'glutton', as his critics asserted, is hard to measure. He was particularly partial to eggs. He ordered five thousand eggs for his Christmas festivities in 1206. He liked chickens too; there is a celebrated entry on a fine roll which says that 'the wife of Hugh de Neville [John's chief forester] gives the lord King 200 chickens that she may lie with her husband for one night'. The exact meaning of this cryptic entry has baffled historians. But John certainly enjoyed a good meal and frequently ignored Lent and other fast days. Because he once ate twice on a Friday, the eve of St Mark's Day, he gave alms to a hundred paupers as a penance.

OPPOSITE A noble lord having a bath in a wooden tub, with the assistance of young ladies. On the right one woman keeps the fire burning with the help of bellows, in order to heat up more water for the tub.

149

An enamelled casket decorated with scenes of country life, made at Limoges in the early thirteenth century.

The Tristram Casket – a wooden casket decorated with ivory or bone plaques carved with scenes from the romance of Tristram and Iseult, dating from about 1200.

John's sex life, which won him the disapproval of Victorian historians as licentious, certainly seems to have been pretty adventurous, though not as adventurous as that of other English kings – Henry I, Henry VIII and Charles II for example – or even perhaps that of his father who lived openly with his mistress, the fair Rosamund. John was betrothed when he was only nine years old to Isabella of Gloucester and he married her in 1189 when he was twenty-one. He divorced her because she had borne him no children or, to be more accurate, the marriage was dissolved because they were second cousins and John – whether deliberately or not – had never troubled to obtain a papal dispensation. In July 1200 he married Isabelle of Angoulême by whom he had two sons and three daughters. He treated neither of his wives badly; after the annulment he often

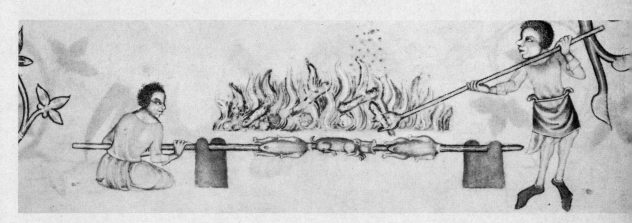

sent presents to his first wife and finally he found her a second husband in the Earl of Essex though the Earl had to pay 20,000 marks for her. His second wife is alleged to have been unfaithful to him, but the evidence is far from solid. John was certainly, and perhaps understandably, unfaithful to his first wife. The names of four of his mistresses and five of his illegitimate children have survived. His illegitimate daughter Joan, as has been seen, was married to Llewelyn the Great of Wales, and his legitimate daughter, Joan, was to marry Alexander II, King of the Scots; two of John's sons served as officers in his army. The story that John importuned and molested the wives and daughters of his barons, including specifically the wives of Eustace de Vesci and Robert fitz Walter, sounds improbable and was no doubt a piece of gossip cooked up by the monks.

The preparation of food:
TOP Cooking with cauldrons;
BELOW Roasting meat on a spit.

John was not irreligious and was at least as good a Christian as his father or eldest brother. It is true that one of the monastic chroniclers, Adam of Eynsham, asserted that John never took the sacraments after he reached manhood, but if his story were true surely it would have been remarked upon by others. Naturally the imposition of the Interdict and the subsequent excommunication damaged John's image with the clergy, secular or monastic. But these were weapons that Innocent III employed pretty indiscriminately – he used them, for example, against both Philip Augustus and Otto IV – and there is no reason to suppose that John had any particular animosity against the Papacy as such; he was simply of the opinion that Innocent III had violated the customary right of the King of England to choose his own archbishop. In the Middle Ages suspicions felt about the conduct of any one Pope were by no means incompatible with a genuine belief in the truth of Christianity.

Although John seized Church property during the Interdict, he did much to temper the harm done to the ordinary clergy by granting them generous allowances; he also trebled the amount of the alms which he was accustomed to give to religious houses. His policy of standing up for what he believed to be his rights met with pretty general approval, which would hardly have been the case if he had been thought to be anti-Christian. He 'seems to have been at least conventionally devout' observes Professor Warren. At the outset of his reign he made a pilgrimage to the shrines of St Thomas Becket, St Alban and St Edmund. In 1200 he paid for the building of an abbey at Beaulieu for the benefit of the Cistercian monks. During the Interdict he borrowed books from the abbot of Reading, though whether he read them is not known. Indeed, at any rate until he was excommunicated, he appears to have been anxious to sustain a reputation for religious orthodoxy.

There was nothing mean about John. One modern historian writes that he was generous to the poor and not ungenerous to the Church. Another says that he was open-handed to his men, liberal to the churches and generous to the poor. He might have been suspicious of his barons, but he was 'indulgent to the proletariat' (Austin Lane Poole). Whenever he violated the religious taboos of his time as by eating meat on a Friday or fishing on a Sunday, he was careful to give alms to the poor by

RIGHT Huntsman with a falcon. Falconry and hawking were popular pastimes among the nobility; the birds were carefully trained and highly prized.

way of penance. When poor people sought justice at his Court, he would lean over backwards to give it to them. To the poor at any rate he sold justice cheaply.

Many adjectives have been applied to John's temper: he is said to have been impatient, passionate, mercurial, unpredictable, harsh, reckless, ruthless, callous, cruel, arrogant, autocratic, capricious, suspicious and to have possessed a biting tongue. Where does the truth lie about all this? Of course the hot temper of the Angevins was notorious and it was unfortunate for John that he inherited his temper from his father. Moreover he had ample reason to be suspicious – the word most frequently used about him – for his barons in both England and France were constantly plotting against him; he had been betrayed more than once in Normandy, in Ireland he had been defied, and in 1212 he was told that his life was in danger from baronial conspirators. A lesser man would have been suspicious in the circumstances.

As to his ruthlessness (which is a less pejorative word than cruelty), rulers have to be ruthless: that is the price that must invariably be paid for exercising and sustaining political supremacy; there can be few or no friends at the top. Most rulers are unable to evade days of the long knives. Ruthlessness is an attribute of modern as well as past rulers from democratic presidents and prime ministers to Communist dictators and eastern monarchs. Possibly John was more mercurial and capricious than other kings. He certainly was hesitant over throwing in his hand after his defeats in 1204 and 1214. But it is likely that he was waiting to see if his luck would change before deciding to conclude peace. John, after all, as has been generally agreed, was rarely lucky.

If John was unstable, if he changed his mind from time to time about how to tackle his problems as king, if he gave way to gusts of anger, it is stretching it rather far to describe him as a manic-depressive. Although it is common for authors to regard their subjects as abnormal, it is never easy to be equable about triumph and disaster and to treat those two imposters just the same.

The paradoxes in John's character have often been pointed out: he was both judicious and extortionate, he was grasping and generous, he was tortuous and determined, he was astute

and reckless, he was unfaithful but not unkind to his wives, he
was brave but could give way to despair. If he was tough with
his baronage, he could be compassionate to the poor. His good
qualities are liable to be overlooked in the torrents of vituper-
ation which have been poured over him by both medieval
chroniclers and historians. Yet his abilities as a statesman, an
administrator, a soldier and a diplomatist were real. To say that
he was a capricious opportunist is absurd. His consistent policy
was to secure peace at home and victory overseas. But that he
was not always successful, genial or level-headed can hardly be
denied.

Was John a cruel tyrant? A number of instances of his cruelty
can be found, including, for instance, his hanging of the Welsh
hostages and the putting to death of the mad prophet Peter of
Wakefield. But these things have to be measured in the context
of the time. It was customary for the lives of hostages to be
forfeit, if those for whom they stood hostage broke their word.
Prophesying the imminent death of the King could understandably be reckoned as treason. The two main reasons for
accusing John of cruelty were first his treatment of Arthur of
Brittany and second his behaviour to the family of William de
Braose. If John really strangled Arthur with his own hands in a
fit of drunken rage and then thrust his body into the river, he
must surely be called cruel. But that story, as has already been
noticed, depends on a single authority which is not strictly
contemporary, and if John simply had Arthur executed as a

154

traitor, he could claim justification. At any rate John never showed the slightest remorse over it. With the case of the De Braoses it is rather different. There the punishment was disproportionate to the crime, although the exact circumstances of the death of Matilda de Braose and her son are by no means clear: indeed their death might have been accidental. John had reason to be suspicious of their conduct, notably when they were with their friends and relatives in Ireland. Nevertheless if Matilda and her son were deliberately starved to death, as the chroniclers aver, then it was an unquestionable act of cruelty. Eight days before he died, John permitted Margaret de Lacy, daughter of William de Braose 'to clear forest land to found a religious house for the salvation of the souls of her father, mother and brother'. Was it contrition? That John was a sadist is extremely doubtful; but that he was as ruthless as his father and at times as violent has to be admitted.

Gerald of Wales wrote that John was the most tyrannous of bloody tyrants. To say that John was a tyrant is to affirm that he was exceptionally arbitrary in his behaviour and that he flouted the laws and customs of the kingdom. John was clearly no more of a tyrant than his father and brother had been, both of whom exploited their customary rights as far as they dared. William I and William II may equally be accused of tyranny. In fact no real constitutional check existed upon the conduct of the Norman or Angevin kings of England who employed every means at their disposal to protect themselves against over-mighty subjects. On the whole John adhered to the rules and accepted the system of justice established by his father. Few or no twentieth-century historians have accused John of tyranny any more than did the strictly contemporary chroniclers. Still, it is not difficult to understand how John acquired such a reputation. The Great Charter (Magna Carta), a feudal compact hastily drawn up in an attempt to effect a reconciliation between the King and his barons during a civil war, was·transmuted during the seventeenth century into a palladium of English liberties which had been extracted from a wicked king. Naturally, those who regarded the Charter in that light assumed that John had been a terrible tyrant. To the real meaning of the sealing of the Charter, which was an episode in the great rebellion against King John, we shall turn in the next chapter.

7 The Great Rebellion

and the Sealing of Magna Carta 1214-16

REBELLION WAS ENDEMIC in medieval England. William the Conqueror had to crush a rebellion in the north; civil war erupted during the reign of King Stephen; John himself had conspired against both his father and his brother. Though fundamentally kings and barons had the same interest in preserving the existing social order, discontented barons could easily be induced to rebel if they believed that they would be better off under another monarch. Thus the central problem for medieval kings was the management of their barons, just as under the Tudors and Stuarts the central problem was to be the management of their Parliaments.

John was fully aware throughout his reign that forces of unrest always lay just beneath the surface of political life. Not only did he know what it was to be a rebel himself but his constant peregrinations around his kingdom, including the visits that he paid almost annually to northern England, had taught him all about the areas and sources of discontent. It was obvious to him that the extraordinary pressures which had been exerted by him and his agents to collect a huge war chest to pay for his allies and mercenaries in the struggle against Philip II of France had created resentment among his leading subjects. He had seen the red light when the plot to murder him was uncovered in August 1212: it was no coincidence that the heads of the conspiracy, who had admitted their guilt by fleeing into exile, were also to be leaders in the great rebellion of 1215.

John took all the steps he reasonably could to prevent a revolutionary outbreak. He had tempered firmness with conciliation. For example, he removed unpopular sheriffs from northern counties and remitted some of his financial claims on those who remained in office. What precisely he said to the unruly northern barons when, after the intervention of Stephen Langton, he met them at Wallingford in November 1213 is not known, but he must have given some promises. He took all the precautions he could to avert unrest at home when he went on campaign in February 1214. Nevertheless, the iron hand exercised by Peter des Roches in the King's absence provoked the barons, who regarded the Justiciar as an upstart and a foreigner. Peter des Roches managed to preserve the peace during 1214, but when John came home, once again defeated in France, he was aware that rebellion was extremely likely.

There were three principal causes of the rebellion in 1215. The first was the unrealised ambitions of disappointed men. Throughout modern history a common source of revolt has been the resentment of men who consider themselves excluded from authority, influence and easy access to wealth – such, for example, as 'the country party' in seventeenth-century England. Of the rebels of 1215 many were barons who thought that they were deliberately and unfairly excluded from royal favours. They saw the King distributing largesse – grants of lands, pensions, profitable wardships and marriages – to others but not to themselves. By bestowing awards on some while dispossessing and disinheriting others, John divided the barons into 'ins' and 'outs'. Offence was felt particularly strongly among the northern barons. 'By and large,' (writes Professor Holt) 'they were "outs", excluded from the spoils of office, despite a family tradition of service to the Crown in many cases, despite the earlier administrative experiences which some of them enjoyed, and despite the expectation of office which their social position gave them.' So they became dissidents and took the opportunity provided by John's defeat abroad to stir up discontent and compel him to acknowledge their grievances or be overthrown.

The second important cause of rebellion was not the grievances of any one particular group but an accumulation of resentment by the whole of the baronage, indeed by nearly all the King's subjects, over the steady increase in John's demands for services and money. That was not peculiar to the reign of John: a sense of outrage had existed under all the Angevins. Henry II, by reorganising the administration of justice, had exerted a tighter hand on the barons and had deprived them of profits from their own jurisdictions. The aids levied by Richard I, first to enable him to go on Crusade and secondly to meet the ransom, upset the entire baronage. On top of that came John's heavy financial requirements to pay for his unsuccessful wars. The enormous sums extorted were frightening. Land-owners, badgered for aids, reliefs and fines, often found difficulty in raising the amounts asked of them. Sometimes they were driven to borrow from the Jews at high rates of interest

The Jews in medieval England

Jews began to settle in England after the Norman
Conquest, but they were generally distrusted and
frequently hated. One of their principal
occupations was money lending. They came
under the protection of the king because he
could lay claim to their properties after
their death.

RIGHT Satire on the Jews from the Roll of
Norwich during the reign of Henry III.
RIGHT BELOW The persecution of the Jews,
carved in stone from Nuremberg Cathedral.

ABOVE Earthenware tile
showing Jews on
the left and Christians
on the right.
RIGHT The destruction
of a synagogue, from a
thirteenth-century
manuscript.

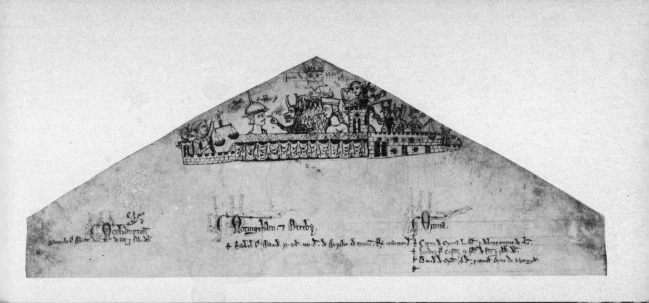

and it was of little use to them to make antisemitic noises because the Jews were officially protected by the King who had a vested interest in them, since debts owed to them reverted to the Crown on their deaths.

The third cause of rebellion was simply an intensification of the second. It was unpleasant enough for the barons that they were obliged to pay feudal dues to their overlord, which were often arbitrary and inconvenient, but they were being constantly made to submit to new forms of taxation over and above the scutages imposed in time of war. For example, the yield of the 'thirteenth' levied on revenues and properties in 1207 far exceeded that from even the highest scutages. The introduction of customs duties was especially irritating to barons who engaged, as many of them often did, in various forms of business enterprise. For example, Eustace de Vesci developed Alnmouth as a port, while Robert de Ros, another northern baron, exported wool and imported wine by way of the Humber River. Throughout the whole of the early history of Europe the exaction of new or higher taxes to pay for wars has been one of the commonest reasons for rebellions.

Such were the underlying causes of the rebellion of 1215. What sparked it off was undoubtedly the demand for scutage at the high rate of three marks per knight's fee which was put forward by John in 1214. It has already been observed how the northern barons refused to serve in Poitou or to pay scutage on the ground that it was contrary to the terms of their tenure. John had been persuaded against his will to give way to them rather than beat it out of them; but when he sailed to France in February 1214 he knew that he had left this recalcitrant group of barons behind him. While he was away Peter des Roches, acting on the King's instructions, attempted to enforce this scutage at the maximum rate, and when in the autumn of 1214 the Exchequer was engaged in trying to collect the money, it met with resistance which spread like wildfire. Neither the barons who served with John in Poitou nor those who stayed at home and refused to pay scutage saw any reason why they should submit to further pressures from a disgraced and defeated King. That was how the battle of Bouvines led directly to the great rebellion of 1215. Indeed the storm clouds might have been detected in the distance when Normandy was lost. The barons submitted to heavy financial pressure under King Richard I, but he at least was victorious. John had been unlucky and was required to pay the penalty.

The malcontents complained that nothing like this had happened in the good old days, that is to say before the Angevins – the Devil's brood – became kings of England. The barons appealed to ancient customs, in particular to the coronation charter of King Henry I and to the laws of Edward the Confessor. Henry I had granted this charter when he was struggling to win popular support. It was couched in pretty vague terms and said nothing about either service abroad or scutage. Its chief importance was that it afforded a precedent for the King committing himself to making concessions by issuing a charter. Undoubtedly Henry I's charter was a talking point among John's barons, but specific stories that their attention was drawn to it by Stephen Langton after he had preached a sermon in St Paul's Cathedral in August 1213, or that it was the subject of discussion at a meeting of barons held in a church at Bury St Edmunds in the autumn of 1214, are more than dubious. The appeal to ancient and agreeable, if fictitious, traditions was the small change of feudal political argument. John could equally appeal to past custom and tradition, though he might not have been able to go so far back. The advantage of such an appeal by barons was that it offered justification for rebellion and enabled them to seek for the abolition of all disagreeable Angevin innovations.

John returned to England from Poitou on 15 October 1214 and immediately a strained situation developed between him and a number of his barons, especially those who had resolutely refused to pay the scutage. These barons now adopted the tactic of appealing from John's methods of government to the customs that prevailed under Henry I, that is to say before the strong-minded Angevins had mounted the English throne. When or where they decided upon this policy is uncertain, but unquestionably it was a concerted movement. According to the Barnwell chronicler, the baronial party produced during the winter of 1214–15 'a certain charter of liberties granted to the English by Henry I', which they sought to have confirmed by John. How this baronial party was made up is not entirely clear. It may have been led by the northerners who had resisted the

'A certain charter of liberties'

A tournament depicted on the side of a French casket, made of ivory. The tournament was a popular form of amusement in the Middle Ages and a useful practice for war.

scutage. At any rate a formal meeting took place in London on 6 January 1215 when John gave a safe conduct to the barons who attended, and they carried arms to the meeting. John was then asked to confirm the charter of Henry I and the laws of Edward the Confessor, but he put off giving his answer until the Sunday after Easter. Meanwhile he renewed his safe conduct to the barons.

164

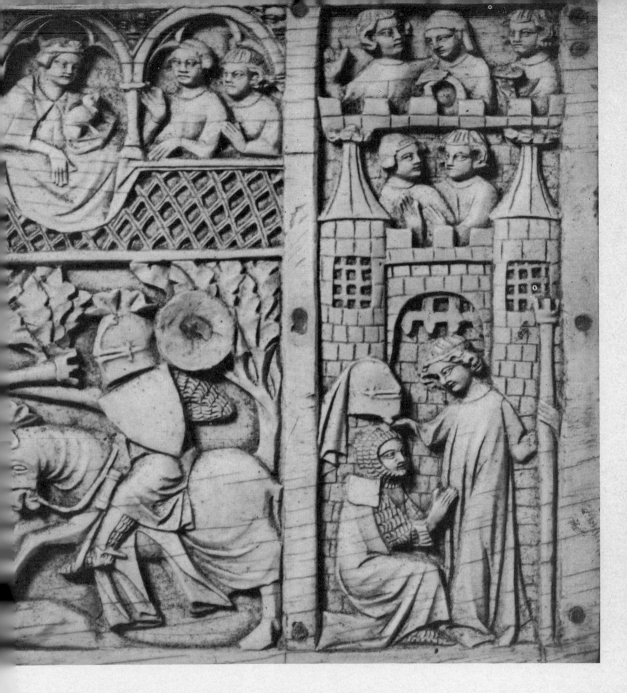

John evidently perceived that rebellion was in the offing. He therefore at once reported the state of affairs to Innocent III, who was now his overlord, and on 4 March (Ash Wednesday), presumably hoping further to ingratiate himself with the Pope, he took an oath as a Crusader. The dissident barons had also made representations at Rome. About the same time or earlier the King called over reinforcements from Poitou. The Pope's reply to John's appeal arrived extremely quickly: letters dated 19 March were sent to John, to the barons and to the Archbishop of Canterbury. It is quite possible that Innocent III, when he wrote them, already knew of John's vow to take the Cross. At any rate, while he asked John to treat the petitions of his barons with sympathy, he told the barons themselves that they must not conspire against their King or try to exact concessions from him by force of arms. Langton, for his part, was reproved for having failed to mediate between John and the dissident barons. On 1 April the Pope sent another letter telling the barons that they must pay the King the scutage that they owed him. Innocent III was utterly determined that nothing should interfere with John's noble design of going upon the Crusade. What was called a 'triple form of peace', which was thus embodied in the Pope's letters, was directed to that end.

John hoped that the matter was now settled and actually countermanded his orders to his friends in Poitou. But the dissident barons were far from satisfied. They proceeded to fortify their castles and to arm themselves for war. At the same time they demanded a reply from the King to their requests which he had promised to give them on 26 April. They mustered at Stamford in Lincolnshire and marched south to Northampton, which was the appointed rendezvous. But the King postponed giving them a reply and instead rallied his adherents in south and south-west England. On 30 April the King was at Wallingford in Berkshire and the barons were at a nearby manor which belonged to one of their number, the Earl of Winchester, 34 miles away. John refused to meet the barons, but sent Stephen Langton, the Archbishop of Canterbury, and William Marshal, Earl of Pembroke, to discover exactly what the demands of these barons were. When John's intermediaries read him their demands, made under the threat of civil war, he absolutely refused to grant them. 'Never would he concede his subjects liberties that would make the king a slave' (Sidney Painter). He added: 'Why not ask for my kingdom?' After these barons learned that their demands had been rejected, they renounced their homage and fealty and defied the King. Robert fitz Walter, Lord of Dunmow, was appointed commander-in-chief of what they called 'the Army of God and the Holy Church', a quaint title for men who were

Effigy of William Longsword, Earl of Salisbury, in Salisbury Cathedral. An illegitimate son of Henry II, he was a trusted friend of his half-brother John, although he deserted the King for a few crucial months when Louis invaded England in 1216.

disobeying the orders of God's representative on earth and were trying to unhorse a dedicated Crusader. The rebels then, on 5 May 1215, marched upon Northampton, but found this important royal castle too well guarded to fall to their assault. In any case they lacked siege weapons. So instead they occupied Bedford, which had been betrayed to them by a sympathiser.

John did not at once retort with war. On the contrary, he offered to submit the differences between himself and his opponents to arbitration with four representatives of each side and the Pope or the Pope's deputy in the chair. Meanwhile he promised to grant 'to our barons who are against us that we shall not arrest them or their men, nor disseise them [confiscate their property] nor turn against them by force or by arms, except by the law of our realm or by the judgment of their peers in our Court'. He further showed goodwill by undertaking to submit fines that he had imposed on two of his enemies, Geoffrey de Mandeville, the titular Earl of Essex, and Giles de Braose, Bishop of Hereford, to the judgment of the Court. But these offers, put forward on 9 and 10 May, were not accepted. The rebels, who must have known that they had put themselves in the wrong, had the bit between their teeth and wanted to fight it out. On 12 May John gave orders that the estates of the rebels should be seized. Thus the civil war began.

Of whom did the sides in the civil war consist? At no time did the rebels command the active support of the entire baronage, although this is one of those popular legends in English history which will never be discarded. In fact in the spring of 1215 only about forty barons can be counted as defying the King, although they were supported by their kindred, their knights and other vassals. Nor is it true, as used to be said, that the rebels were exclusively northerners, although the northerners were certainly important. They included, besides Eustace de Vesci, William de Mowbray, who was said to be 'as small as a dwarf' and commanded the service of seventy-eight knights, Roger de Montbegon, who held lands in Lancashire, Robert de Ros and Robert Grelley, Lord of Manchester, both of whom owned property in Lincolnshire, and Gilbert de Gant, who had a claim to the earldom of Lincoln and boasted the service of sixty-nine knights. De Vesci and De Ros were both brothers-in-law of Alexander II, King of the Scots. But 'although at its

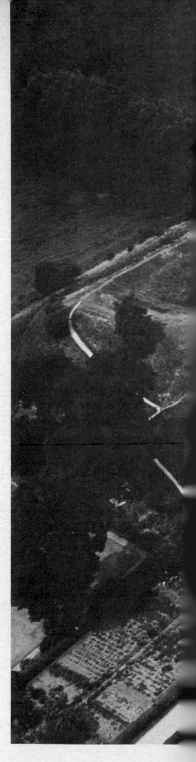

Framlingham Castle in Suffolk built by
Roger Bigod, Earl of Norfolk in the 1190s.
In 1216 the castle was besieged and taken
by King John and his army.

RIGHT The Charter of
King John to the
City of London on
9 May 1215. It included
the right of the City to
elect its own mayor.

OPPOSITE The Bell Tower
in the Tower of London,
built during the reign of
King John.

height the rebellion came to include a formidable proportion
of the baronage of the northern counties' (J. C. Holt), John also
had loyal supporters there: he himself was Earl of Lancaster
and he could count on the allegiance of Ranulf, Earl of Chester
and William de Ferrers, Earl of Derby. Towards the end of his
reign John experienced little difficulty in exercising military
control over the north of England. The area commanded by
the northern rebels was by no means geographically solid nor
were they united by any cause except a sense of personal
grievance against the King, owing to their failures in litigation
or their ill success in purchasing favours.

Others of the leading rebel barons were associated with
eastern England and included their commander-in-chief,
Robert fitz Walter, whose lands lay largely in Essex, his son-in-
law, Geoffrey de Mandeville, Earl of Essex, and Roger Bigod,
Earl of Norfolk. They also had some supporters in south-western
England. But the notion that the rebels were younger men than

170

The Sealing of Magna Carta

BELOW LEFT The Articles of the Barons in which the barons presented their demands to King John. Magna Carta was based partly on this document.

RIGHT Runnymede, where John met the barons to arrange the final terms of Magna Carta. The Charter ends with the words 'Given in the meadow that is called Runnymede between Windsor and Staines, 15 June.'

BELOW RIGHT The Great Charter of June 1215 – a famous document in English history.

John's adherents does not appear to be true: their leaders were mainly in their forties.

The King, besides his friends in the north, particularly in Cheshire, could rely on William Marshal, Earl of Pembroke, to whom he was fully reconciled (though William's son fought as a rebel), and the Earls of Salisbury, Warwick, Devon and Surrey. John's strength therefore lay mainly in southern and western England and to some extent in the midlands and Cheshire. John's baronial adherents were nearly all wealthy, sagacious and experienced men. Between the two sides can be discerned a body of neutralists or powerful families who were divided among themselves, just as the rebels against King Charles I were to be. Thus the idea that it was 'the barons of England' who fought King John and compelled him to seal the Great Charter is completely untenable. If any one group propelled him in that direction it was the neutralists who, under the hard-working guidance of Stephen Langton, attempted to harmonise the King's traditional rights with 'the restatement of English custom in the light of new necessities' (Maurice Powicke).

John might have crushed the rebellion, if he had wanted to, by purely strong-arm methods. Many of the strategic castles were in his hands, and he asked Stephen Langton to surrender to him the castle at Rochester which lay between London and the south coast, where it was possible that help for the rebels might arrive from France. He also had at his disposal both Poitevin and Flemish mercenaries. In order not to be provocative he had stationed the Poitevin mercenaries under the command of Savaric de Mauléon in Ireland. While the rebels had been vainly trying to besiege Northampton, John ordered the Earl of Salisbury and the Flemish mercenaries to occupy London, while he called over De Mauléon and his Poitevins to Winchester where they would be available to guard the south coast. However, the rebels, after taking hold of Bedford, marched on London and arrived there before the Earl of Salisbury. John had granted an extremely favourable charter to the citizens of London a week before and the majority of Londoners were royalists. But a minority opened the gates of the capital to the rebels on Sunday 17 May. They plundered the City, confiscating the property of the Jews and pulling down their houses.

The Wool Industry

A large amount of wool was exported from
England in early times and English wool was
known for its high quality. Although wool was
spun within the home, as it was the foundation
for the average person's clothes, it was not until
the twelfth century, with the immigration of
skilled Flemish weavers, that the cloth-
manufacturing industry began to develop. By the
early thirteenth century the industry was in a
flourishing condition.

RIGHT A shepherd and his flock.
BELOW Winding skeins and weaving on an
upright loom.

Agriculture in the Middle Ages

In spite of wars, life for the common people went on in comparative quiet. Each villein (or unfree tenant farmer) had to work for his lord for some days of the week, and in time of harvest, but the rest of the time, he could cultivate his own plot of land, from which he had to support his family.

RIGHT ABOVE Woman milking a cow (Bodleian Ms 175 M.B. f.41v)
RIGHT BELOW Bees flying into a hive (Bodleian Roll 189A f.111V)

ABOVE Cutting corn with a sickle.
LEFT Threshing with a flail.
BELOW Woman feeding chickens.

ar monent innite. mme mrdilline 7 mite sut. Qxe
e ab agris dite negante quidā carnes latrare quibz m
i mma mmca firn datu dr mma.

Hubert de Burgh, created
Chief Justiciar of England
in June 1215, after the
sealing of Magna Carta.

Nevertheless the King's partisans held out in the Tower of London.

According to Roger of Wendover, the rebels in London sent an appeal to the barons who remained loyal to the King urging them to join in the rebellion and threatening them with war and destruction as 'public enemies' if they failed to do so. John played for time. He evidently felt that since the rebels had occupied the capital and were engaged on besieging the Tower, and since reports started reaching him of other rebel outbreaks both in the south-west of his kingdom and in the Midlands, he had better agree to a truce and to the opening of negotiations. On 27 May he asked Stephen Langton, who was trusted by both sides, to arrange a truce and the mercenaries were ordered to observe it. Two days later he again wrote to the Pope outlining his efforts at reconciliation and complaining of the behaviour of the rebel barons who were preventing him from going on the Crusade.

What precisely happened during the next fortnight is by no means perfectly clear, but it appears that the rebels did not observe the truce and that John called up more mercenaries, this time from Wales. But Stephen Langton, William Marshal and other mediators took energetic action. They rode backwards and forwards between the King, who had moved from his headquarters in Wiltshire to Windsor, and the barons in London. John was persuaded to give a safe conduct to all those who wished to do so to come to Staines on behalf of the barons, and on 15 June 1215 he met them to conclude a negotiated peace in a meadow called Runnymede on the banks of the Thames between Windsor and Staines.

A grand formal ceremony must have taken place at Runnymede on 15 June, for that was the date inscribed on the celebrated charter which was issued by John and was the outcome of the negotiations between the King and his barons. According to the chronicler Ralph of Coggeshall, 'by the intervention of the Archbishop of Canterbury and some barons, a sort of peace was made'. That peace had indeed come and that the rebellion had been brought to an end was evidently accepted by all those who gathered at Runnymede on 15 June. But in fact the negotiations neither began nor ended upon that day. The King is known to have been at Runnymede as early as 10 June and it was probably then that the King and the rebel barons, who had not yet arrived at Runnymede, through the mediation of the Archbishop and a number of suffragan bishops, consented to draft terms; these have survived in a document

Magna Carta Indenture of 1215: an agreement between King John and the earls, barons and freemen of the realm, that they should hold London while oaths were taken throughout the country according to the Charter of Liberties of June 1215.

C omer vivien˜ fu fais chevalier ·

S eignoȝ baron p̃ dieu oȝ entendeȝ
J ceste estoire · iames meillor voȝreȝ
C est de · G · le marchis au coȝt neȝ
L e meillor home q̃ de mie fuȝt neȝ
S e qui des armes peust plus endurer
O ne ne fina la sele graⁿȝ boⁿȝeȝ

The Age of Knighthood

For ambitious young men in early
medieval England the path to wealth and
power lay through tournaments and
knighthood. The reality of the knight's
life was removed from the romantic
cult of chivalry which grew up in the
later Middle Ages.

OPPOSITE
LEFT With hands upraised to take the
oath, two squires are girt with the
sword of knighthood.
RIGHT The romantic view of knighthood
– a knight with his lady.

BELOW Squire being dubbed a knight
by his king and presented with his
shield and banner.

called 'the articles of the barons' which afterwards lay hidden for five hundred years in the archives of Canterbury Cathedral. The draft articles were sealed with the Great Seal and this provided a guarantee to the rebels that the negotiations were seriously intended. By 15 June therefore the draft articles were accepted by both sides and it was agreed that the final terms should be worked out. Details were arranged and the Chancery clerks produced a magnificent document of which four copies survive, with the date 15 June inscribed on them. On 19 June the peace was 'made firm', the King's agents were ordered to refrain from any further acts of war, and some, but apparently not all, of the rebel barons renewed their homage to John.

What did the Charter contain? It was compounded of many strands, but its most remarkable characteristic was that it was extremely comprehensive. 'It was granted,' writes Professor Holt, 'to all freemen throughout the realm'; and even unfree tenants or villeins are mentioned in clause 20; fines were not to be so heavy that they were deprived of their means of livelihood. The tenants-in-chief promised to treat their own free tenants in the same way that the King undertook to treat them. Liberties were thus won for the freemen of England as a whole. It was mainly to Archbishop Stephen Langton, who throughout acted as the mediator or moderator between the King and his barons, that the broad character of the settlement was owed.

The rebel barons, in attempting to force concessions from King John, had appealed to the customs of the past – largely a fictitious past – and had looked back to the good old days before the Angevins came to power. Thus the Charter purported to abolish 'evil customs' that had grown up, to set out the existing law, and also to state what it was hoped would now become law 'by glossing customs so that the Charter was made relevant to the circumstances of the day'. Finally, John ensured that the provisions of the Charter would become a permanent part of the law of the land by allowing (clause 61) the barons to elect twenty-five of their number who should (in John's words) 'with their utmost power keep, hold and cause to be kept the peace and liberties which we have granted unto them and by this our present Charter have confirmed'. If the articles of peace were broken, then the twenty-five barons were entitled to lay hold of the King's castles, lands and possessions until compensation had been secured. In other words, an enduring right of rebellion was permitted by the Charter. That was one of the most astonishing features of the settlement of 15 June 1215.

The sixty-three clauses of the Charter defined the liberties of the community. The way in which the King was allowed to obtain his recognised feudal dues was set out. The King's rights with regard to reliefs on the succession of heirs, wardships, marriages of tenants-in-chief or their widows and services for knights' fees were defined. No scutages or aids, with certain exceptions which had to be 'reasonable', could be imposed except by the common counsel of the kingdom. Restrictions were placed on the exploitation of debts owed to the Jews, and certain Poitevins were removed from the King's service. Promises were made by John about the organisation of justice: for example, it was stated that 'Common Pleas shall not follow Our Court but shall be held in some fixed place' and limitations were sought on the use of the writ *praecipe*. The King's forests, which had their own strict laws that caused resentment, especially among poachers, were the subject of three clauses of the Charter; all 'evil customs' were to be abolished. Other clauses referred to the liberties of the Church, of the City of London and of foreign merchants who came to England to trade. The most famous clauses of the Charter, which were frequently to be quoted in the course of English history, were clauses 39 and 40. Clause 39 provided that 'No man shall be taken, imprisoned, outlawed, banished or in any way destroyed, nor will we proceed against or prosecute him except by the lawful judgment of his peers [his equals] or by the law of the land.' Clause 40 pronounced in a grand way: 'To no one will we sell, to no one will we deny or delay, right or justice.'

What the Charter contained therefore was a statement (though it was neither entirely clear nor complete) of the laws and liberties of England. Just as the Grand Remonstrance of 1641 was to set out the grievances felt against King Charles I by his subjects and the Bill of Rights was to set out the grievances felt against King James II by his, so the Charter of 1215 was a commentary on the behaviour of King John and the earlier Angevin kings.

But the Great Charter – the Magna Carta, which was to

'To no one will we ...deny or delay right or justice'

become so famous in English history and indeed in the history of the English-speaking world – was not John's Charter of 1215 but a charter granted by Henry III, John's son and successor. In November 1216 a charter which was first issued in his name when some of the clauses obnoxious to the monarchy – such as the standing committee of twenty-five barons – were deleted. In 1217 this charter was again reissued and again modified: in particular, clauses relating to the royal forests were withdrawn, expanded and included in a second, smaller forest charter, issued in the same year. It was because the forest charter of 1217 was a little one and the other revised charter was a big one that when these two charters were reissued in 1225 (by the goodwill of the young Henry III in return for a grant of money by his barons and free tenants), the latter became known as 'the Great Charter' – Magna Carta. It was that charter, the charter of 1225, and not John's Charter, which was quoted with so much veneration by Edward Coke and other famous seventeenth-century figures as 'the law of laws' of such fundamental significance that royal letters patent could not touch it.

John's Charter had no such significance: it was no 'palladium of liberties' valid for all time. It was a strictly feudal document, reactionary in parts, which could never have been enforced, for it pointed the road to political anarchy. One modern historian (Frank Barlow) has described it as 'an inadequate judgment on the past and an impracticable guide for the future'; another (Austin Lane Poole) wrote: 'for John's reign the constitutional importance of Magna Carta is negligible. Its importance lay in the future.' The contemporary biographer of William Marshal, one of the protagonists of the Charter, does not even mention it in the poetic life that he wrote about his hero. William Shakespeare, who depended chiefly on the chronicles of Raphael Holinshed, written in the reign of Queen Elizabeth I, does not refer to the sealing of the Charter in his play *King John*; for him the highlight of the reign was the death of Arthur of Brittany. So far as John's reign is concerned, the scene at Runnymede was simply an incident or episode in a feudal contest. The issuing of the Charter was an excuse for concluding peace in a civil war. But neither side in fact abided by it.

After the famous gathering at Runnymede, John appeared to turn over a new leaf. Not only did he order that sealed copies

OPPOSITE Part of the keep of Rochester Castle in Kent. The round tower of the keep was rebuilt after John had destroyed the original square tower during his siege in 1215. The other three towers are all the original square towers dating from the twelfth century. John finally captured the castle in October 1215.

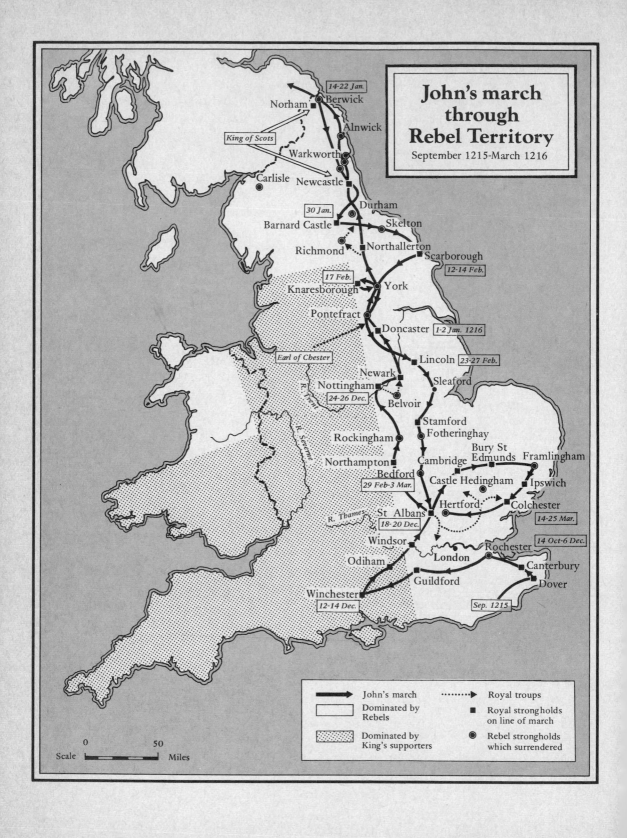

John's march through Rebel Territory
September 1215–March 1216

14-22 Jan.
Norham
Berwick
Alnwick
King of Scots
Warkworth
Carlisle
Newcastle
30 Jan.
Durham
Barnard Castle
Skelton
Richmond
Northallerton
Scarborough
12-14 Feb.
17 Feb.
Knaresborough
York
Pontefract
Doncaster
1-2 Jan. 1216
Earl of Chester
Lincoln
23-27 Feb.
Newark
Sleaford
Nottingham
24-26 Dec.
Belvoir
Stamford
Fotheringhay
Rockingham
Bury St
Edmunds
Framlingham
Northampton
Cambridge
Ipswich
Bedford
Castle Hedingham
Colchester
29 Feb-3 Mar.
Hertford
14-25 Mar.
R. Thames
St Albans
18-20 Dec.
Rochester
14 Oct-6 Dec.
Windsor
London
Canterbury
Odiham
Guildford
Dover
Winchester
12-14 Dec.
Sep. 1215

R. Trent
R. Severn

Scale 0 ___ 50 ___ Miles

➤ John's march	┈➤ Royal troops
☐ Dominated by Rebels	■ Royal strongholds on line of march
▨ Dominated by King's supporters	◉ Rebel strongholds which surrendered

of the Charter should be distributed to every shire but he instructed his sheriffs and foresters and all the royal bailiffs to take oaths of loyalty to the twenty-five barons who had been elected as a watch-dog committee. He appointed Hubert de Burgh, a baron who had played an important part at Runnymede and was trusted by both sides, to replace the unpopular Peter des Roches as Chief Justiciar, and he selected several new sheriffs in substitution for others who were disliked by the dissident barons. The King also went out of his way to settle the case of a number of his subjects who claimed that they had been treated arbitrarily by him or by his predecessors, having been deprived of their lands, castles or privileges without the judgment of their peers (as provided in clause 39 of the Charter). Satisfied that peace had now been attained, John commanded the foreign mercenaries who had been concentrated at Dover to return home.

The more extreme barons were, however, not prepared to trust the King. According to the Barnwell annalist, one of the more reliable if confusing chroniclers, some of the barons had actually left Runnymede even before the firm peace was agreed on 19 June and therefore did not consider themselves bound by it. They set about fortifying castles which they had recovered from the King's officers and refused to give security to be loyal in the future. Moreover, the barons who had been occupying London refused to give it up. They demanded that the Tower of London should be placed in the hands of one of their number, Geoffrey de Mandeville, Earl of Essex, and they insisted that they should retain control of the capital in the King's name until 15 August and that they should keep it longer if they were not satisfied by then of the King's genuine intention to fulfil his promises. They invited William d'Aubigny, Lord of Belvoir, whose loyalty to the King was shaky, to reinforce them in the defence of London and they arranged to move a big tournament originally planned for Stamford so that it should be held a week later more conveniently at Staines. The victor's prize, according to the unreliable Roger of Wendover, was to be 'a bear, which a lady is going to send': not, it might be thought, a very attractive prize, and it is likely that the tournament was really designed to give cover to fresh military preparations by the barons in London.

OPPOSITE The head of
the effigy of King John,
made about twenty
years after his death,
in Worcester Cathedral.

Some of the barons invited John to meet them in Oxford a
month after the assembly at Runnymede to provide for the
general pacification of the country and to clear up imprecisions
in the Charter which was vague about several matters. John
duly attended the meeting, although he arrived late because he
had been struck down with gout, and some sort of a convention
was agreed. But when Langton and the other bishops who had
been acting as mediators proposed a further meeting in Oxford
in the second half of August John had become suspicious and
refused by going there to put himself in the power of barons
who, he rightly said, had treated him badly ever since the con-
clusion of peace. By that time too his overlord, the Pope, had
intervened.

John had sound reason for feeling suspicious because of the
way in which some of the barons were fortifying their castles
and even building new ones, and because of their refusal to
move out of London. In the first half of August therefore he
decided to mobilise a fresh army: he recalled the Flemings,
whom he had dispersed, he tried to raise troops in Brittany and
Aquitaine, and he also wooed the nobility in Ireland, no doubt
with a view to their offsetting disloyalty in England. He hoped
that his forces would be ready by Michaelmas (29 September)

BELOW Two groups of
bishops disputing at the
ecumenical council at
the Lateran held by
Innocent III in 1213.

188

after the harvest had been gathered in. Finally, some time in July or August – possibly after his visit to Oxford in mid-July – John sent a message to Pope Innocent III inviting him to annul the Charter. His appeal to the Pope was a violation of the Charter (clause 61) which specifically stated that:

> We will procure nothing from anyone, either personally or through anyone else, whereby any of the concessions and liberties may be revoked or diminished; and if any such thing be procured, let it be null and void, and it shall never be made use of either by ourselves or by anyone else.

These words were clearly inserted by the barons with the object of preventing the Pope, as John's overlord, from cancelling the Charter.

Thus in the second half of August 1215 both sides were

The shipwreck of Hugh de Boves in the autumn of 1215. De Boves, an organiser of mercenary armies, was drowned when his ships, bringing Flemish soldiers to fight for King John in the civil war, were overwhelmed by a storm.

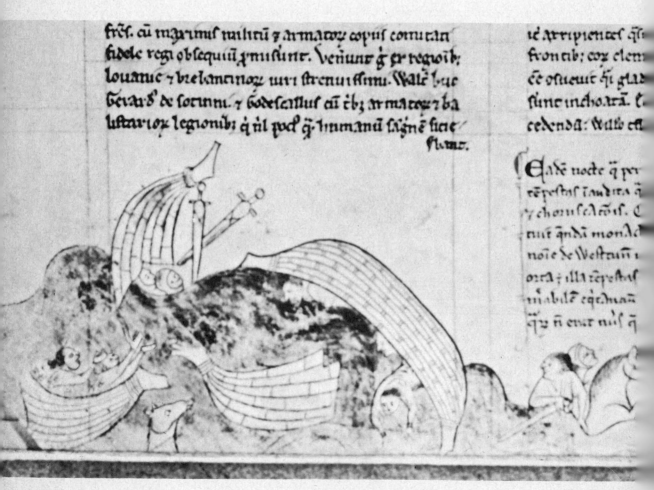

getting ready to renew the civil war. On 16 August a mandate was received from Pope Innocent III addressed to the legate Pandulf, Peter des Roches, Bishop of Winchester and the Abbot of Reading as his appointed commissioners in reply to the letter that John had sent to him on 29 May (more than a fortnight before the formal meeting at Runnymede), expressing great indignation at the way in which the barons were treating their King and ordering that all 'disturbers of the King and kingdom of England' should be excommunicated and an Interdict also placed on their lands; the sentence on the barons was to be published every Sunday and every festival day with the tolling of bells and with candles extinguished until the wrongs they had done to the King were righted. If the Archbishop of Canterbury or any other bishops failed to carry out these

Prince Louis, the son of Philip Augustus, on his way to invade England in May 1216, from the Chronicle of Matthew Paris.

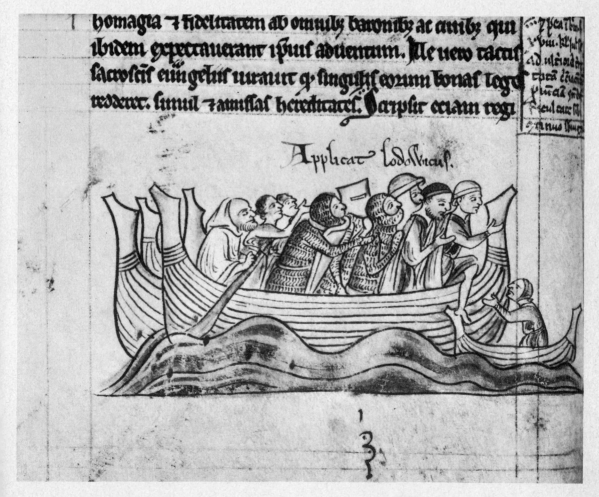

measures, they were on the Pope's instructions to be suspended from office.

The commissioners, after consulting the bishops, decided not to put the Pope's mandate into immediate effect, first on the ground that it was vague and named nobody, and secondly in the hope that a fresh meeting could still be arranged between John and his barons to clear up any misunderstanding arising out of the peace settlement. A proposal was put forward for a conference at Staines, but John was by then too distrustful to agree to further negotiations, all the more so since the barons in London still refused to surrender control of the City to him. In fact it seems certain that the rebel barons again formally defied the King about the end of August. The King therefore took action at once. After leaving the Queen and her eldest son (the future Henry III) in Corfe Castle, John set out to sea on a tour of inspection of the southern ports and then landed at Dover to await the gathering of his new army.

By the end of August the Pope's commissioners decided that they had no alternative but to obey their orders and on 5 September they pronounced the sentences of excommunication and Interdict, though they named no names. Some of the dissident barons insolently asserted that John himself was the principal 'disturber of the peace'. Stephen Langton, terribly disappointed that all his efforts to procure a general conciliation had gone for nothing, refused to publish the sentence of excommunication and was suspended from office by the papal commissioners. He then resolved to go to Rome so that he could tell the Pope the truth about the events in England as he saw them. But other envoys sailed for Rome at the same time to put the King's side of the case. Langton was so depressed that he thought of resigning his see and becoming a monk or a hermit. He obtained no comfort in Rome. Even before he arrived there Innocent III had by a bull dated 24 August annulled the Charter as 'vile and base' and in November the Pope upheld his commissioners' suspension of Langton from his offices.

The Pope's annulment of the Charter was made known in England at the end of September 1215. That was the signal for the resumption of the civil war for which both sides had been preparing. The castle of Rochester, which John had returned to Langton after the settlement at Runnymede, had been seized

OPPOSITE The King John Cup – traditionally part of the King's treasure, most of which was lost in the Wellstream after he marched from King's Lynn to Newark. The cup is now in the Guildhall at King's Lynn.

The Upper Chapel in the keep of Dover Castle. Hubert de Burgh successfully defended the castle against attacks by Louis of France in the spring of 1216.

on the orders of the barons in London who persuaded William d'Aubigny to come south and take it under his command with a picked band of knights. John regarded it as essential to capture this castle so as to clear the route to London from the south. At the same time he instructed his half-brother, the Earl of Salisbury, to collect a field army from the garrisons in the royal castles; he himself was content with a small force to besiege Rochester. There is a story that one of John's Flemish allies expressed his surprise at this, saying: 'You make little account of your enemies if you go to fight them with so small a force.' 'I know them well,' retorted John, 'they are to be nothing accounted or feared. With fewer men than we have we might safely fight them.' John ordered up siege weapons and commanded all the smiths in Canterbury to set to work making pickaxes. But the castle was extremely strong and would not yield to bombardment, mining or assault. Nevertheless, the castle was poorly provisioned and the barons in London failed either to relieve it or to send in supplies. The siege began on 11 October and seven weeks later William d'Aubigny surrendered under threat of starvation. John was with difficulty dissuaded from hanging the entire garrison.

It was a notable victory, for other rebel castles soon followed the example of Rochester and surrendered. The clique of barons in London, headed by Geoffrey de Mandeville, was almost reduced to despair. They decided that the only thing they could do was to appeal to the King of France for help. They therefore invited Philip II's son and heir, Louis, to depose John and assume the Crown of England, thus 'plucking them out of the hand of the tyrant'. Louis was in fact married to John's niece, Blanche of Castile, but this was not a main factor in the situation. More important was the attitude of the King of France. The rebels were content, if they could obtain his military backing, to overthrow John and afterwards make up their minds what was best to be done next.

Philip Augustus was both shrewd and cautious. He had no wish again to tangle with the Pope, who was John's overlord. Indeed Innocent III had sent a legate (named Gualo) through France especially in order to help King John. However, King Philip was anxious not to miss any opportunity of overthrowing his old enemy. He therefore informed the papal legate that John had never been the rightful King of England: he had been condemned for treason at the Court of King Richard I and the murdered Arthur of Brittany had been the lawful heir. Louis, for his part, maintained that his father was only his liege lord in France and no one could prevent him from pursuing his wife's claim, as the grand-daughter of King Henry II, to the English throne. In the spring of 1216 Louis started sending his knights across the Channel to England.

Meanwhile, since the capture of Rochester, John had been pressing forward in his fight against the rebels, even though winter was approaching fast. After holding a council at St Albans on 20 December 1215 John had resolved to divide his army. He ordered the Earl of Salisbury, assisted by two of the most trusted mercenary captains, Falkes de Bréauté and Savaric

'Plucking them out of the hand of the tyrant'

The interior of the Cathedral at St Albans, showing the Norman arches at the crossing. St Albans, standing on the Great North Road and being close to London, was a centre of political life during this period. It was in this abbey that the two monks who wrote chronicles of King John's reign worked.

de Mauléon, to contain the rebel barons in London, while he himself campaigned in the midlands and northern England, laying waste the castles and lands of his enemies. From St Albans John advanced to Northampton and thence to Nottingham where he spent Christmas. In January 1216 he was in Yorkshire and thence he marched towards Scotland promising that he would revenge himself on the young King Alexander II, the 'little red fox cub' as John called him, who owed a debt of gratitude to the English King but had thrown in his lot with the rebel barons. In mid-January 1216 John captured the town and castle of Berwick-upon-Tweed, which he set on fire, and then swept on as far north as Dunbar. By the end of the month he turned south and spent most of February and March harrying East Anglia. Meanwhile John's other army had been active in the home counties around London, but neither army was able to shake the rebels' hold on the capital. In fact John got no nearer than Enfield, 12 miles north-east of London, and after he had carried out a reconnaissance, he skirted the capital and returned to his castle at Windsor.

In the spring John was obliged to concern himself with the threatened invasion from France. He therefore concentrated his army in Kent and gave orders for all the southern and eastern ports to dispatch ships to Dover. He envisaged himself sailing with a fleet across the Channel so as to bottle up Prince Louis in Calais. But on 18 May John's fleet was scattered or destroyed in a storm and two days later Prince Louis landed safely in England. Leaving Dover under the command of his new Justiciar, Hubert de Burgh, John himself withdrew to Winchester there to await developments.

The unopposed landing of the French had startling consequences. King Alexander II plucked up courage again to cross the Scottish border and some of John's adherents, including the Earls of Surrey and York and, most serious of all, his half-brother, the Earl of Salisbury, who had hitherto been so reliable, soon went to Prince Louis's camp to do homage. Prince Louis was by then laying siege to Winchester where he failed to catch John who had returned westwards. The English King had left in command Savaric de Mauléon, who set the city on fire before he departed to join his master. That was in the middle of June, but before then Louis had entered London which he reinforced with French troops and where he received a rapturous welcome from his barons and citizens. After leaving Winchester Louis decided to take personal charge of the siege of Dover, for it was essential that he should keep open his line of communications with France.

For the time being John remained in the west of England perambulating the country from Wiltshire to the borders of Wales, west of Herefordshire, and watching the course of events. Although it has been estimated that two-thirds of the baronage had by then thrown in their lot with Prince Louis, who proclaimed himself but had not yet been crowned King of England, John was not without stout and faithful friends. William the Marshal, now about seventy, and Ranulf, Earl of Chester, secured the west midlands for him and Hubert de Burgh defied Louis from Dover Castle. Moreover, some of John's old enemies were dead: Eustace de Vesci was killed while assisting the King of the Scots in a hopeless siege in County Durham, Geoffrey de Mandeville was accidently killed at a tournament and William Longsword, Earl of Salisbury, renewed his loyalty to his half-brother.

By the beginning of September 1216 John considered that the rot had been stopped and resolved to undertake the offensive

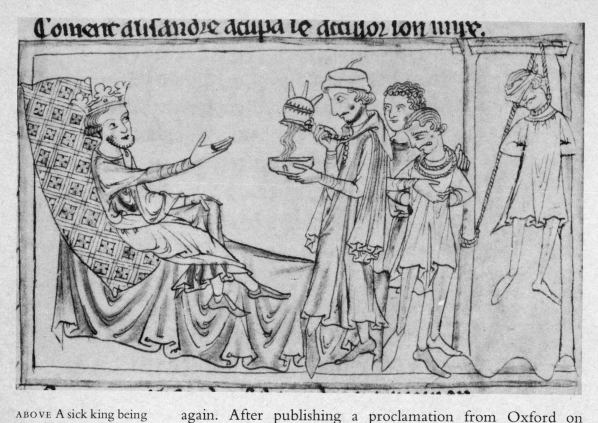

Coment alifandie acupa le dragoz lon mue.

ABOVE A sick king being administered a hot potion. On the right a man has been hanged, while another is led away.

OPPOSITE Newark Castle, the home of the bishop of Lincoln, where King John died on 18 October 1216.

again. After publishing a proclamation from Oxford on 3 September rallying his supporters in southern England, he took Cambridge from the rebel barons a fortnight later and then advanced through Huntingdonshire into Lincolnshire, aiming to subdue the whole of eastern England, cutting off his enemies in the north from those in the south. After relieving Lincoln, which had been nobly defended on his behalf by the dame of the castle, at the end of September, John turned south-east and received a warm welcome from the citizens of King's Lynn. But while he was there the result of much hard riding and over-eating was to bring him down with dysentery. On 11 October however he moved south-west to Wisbech and next day pushed on towards Swineshead Abbey. To reach the abbey John had to cross the old River Ouse (or the Wellstream, as it was then known) which flowed out into the Wash; his baggage train, carrying his treasure and jewels, followed slowly behind. The aim was to negotiate the mouth of the river estuary, which was $4\frac{1}{2}$ miles wide, at low tide. But in the autumn mists which hung over the fenlands, the wagons lost their way,

198

were trapped in the quicksands and then were overwhelmed by a rush of waters returning from the sea. John himself awaited his wagons on the northern side of the river, but when he rode back to help he found there was nothing he could do. According to Roger of Wendover, 'the ground opened in the midst of the waters and whirlpools sucked in everything, men and horses'.

When John at last reached Swineshead Abbey, sick and distressed, he is said to have worsened his fever by supping too greedily on peaches and new cider. Next day he reached Sleaford to the west; here his temper was not improved by the arrival of messengers from Hubert de Burgh saying that he had been compelled to agree to a truce at Dover. From Sleaford the King set out on horseback, moving farther west, impelled by a restless energy, though he could scarcely drag himself along, aiming for the Bishop of Lincoln's castle at Newark, which looks out upon the River Trent. There for three days John lay dying, tended by the Abbot of Croxton, who had a reputation for medical skill, but he could do nothing for the King except perform the last religious rites. Before John died he dictated a will. He named the papal legate, Gualo, Peter des Roches, Bishop of Winchester, William the Marshal (from

Side-view of the effigy of King John in Worcester Cathedral. In his will, which he dictated shortly before his death, he requested that his 'body be buried in the church of the Blessed Virgin and St Wulfstan at Worcester'.

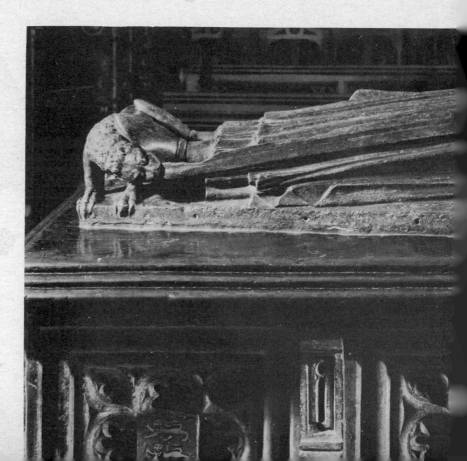

whom he asked forgiveness) and Ranulf of Chester, together with his two faithful mercenary captains, Savaric de Mauléon and Falkes de Bréauté, and others as his executors. They were instructed to 'make satisfaction to God and the Holy Church for the wrongs I have done them,' to send help to the Holy Land, to assist his sons in the recovery and defence of their inheritance, to reward those who had served him loyally and to distribute alms to the poor and to religious houses for the salvation of his soul. He had already declared his eldest son, Henry, to be his heir and had commended him to the guardianship of William the Marshal. John asked that his body should be interred at the church of the Blessed Virgin and St Wulfstan, his patron saint, in Worcester.

The King's last requests were to be fulfilled. A funeral procession, guarded by men in armour, embarked on the long journey south-westwards from Newark to Worcester, where the Bishop buried John according to his wishes. An epitaph by a poet has been preserved:

> In this tomb lies buried a monarch's outward form,
> Who dying stilled upon earth war's tumultuous storm.

...petum irruencium sustinere ñ potuit. hortatu
redderet. ut uiuus euade posset. At ille cū uir
horribili affirmauit q̈ se anglicis alicui
dderet cū q̄ p̄m̄ regis proditores fuerunt.
ditis irruit quidam de regalibz ⁊ p ocul
cor ut ei̍ pforando cerebrū effudit ⁊ t̄lit
bᵓū sepe peioꝛauit. Et corruens in ēram ſ̄
cauit nec ꝟbum unū edidit. S; ꝺ sūmo ra
ad inferos peginauit. Videntes igꝶ gall
maior coꝛ ꝑs cecidiſſ; inierunt fugā tū
equites sibi nimis dapnosam. Nam fla
austral' ꝑ q̄n fugerunt q̄ ex transiliſſo
catū: fugientes ñ mediocꝶ ꝭpediuit. Et
eūꝗ aliⱥſ aduenienſ ⁊ festinuſ nimis g
ſet: opoꝛtebat eum ab equo descende ⁊ po
quo exeunte poꝛta statī recludebaꝶ flag

comes p̄to

8

The Achievement of King John 1199-1216

UNQUESTIONABLY JOHN was an extremely maligned king. It is doubtful if the legends which have encrusted his memory will ever be entirely dispersed. There are many reasons for this, but the most important are three: the first is the stories by the monastic chroniclers, nearly all of whom have been shown by modern research to be completely unreliable in what they said about John, because their works were largely compiled out of gossip and rumour directed against a monarch who had alienated the Church and aspersed the clergy. Yet there can be little doubt that John was a sincere Christian according to the standards of his time. Secondly, John was contrasted with his father and brother, both of whom enjoyed inflated reputations. But if one studies the writings of Gerald of Wales, one perceives that however competent and original an administrator Henry II might have been, in his private life and his behaviour towards his barons, he was far more out-rageous than his son, who may have been 'feckless' in his youth, but after he became King of England, 'took a thoroughly intelligent and immensely energetic interest in the running of the country' (J. C. Holt). Thirdly, when John died he left his kingdom in a state of chaos. Having lost most of his hold on France and having been forced to acknowledge that by a series of truces, he had permitted his old enemy Philip Augustus to turn the tables on him by allowing his son Louis to invade England and link up with the dissident English barons. When John died, they occupied half the shires of England and controlled the whole of the south coast except Dover. The heritage of John's son, the nine-year-old Henry III, seemed to be doomed to destruction.

However, it must be remembered that the reigns of most medieval kings closed in ruin. William the Conqueror died after having been compelled to abandon his campaign in Normandy, against his French overlord, away from England where he was little loved. William II was killed by an arrow while hunting in the New Forest and his body was afterwards carted away by peasants to an unceremonious burial. Henry I died, like his father, fighting in Normandy to quell a rebellion instigated by his daughter and son-in-law, leaving England a prey to anarchy. Henry II and Richard I also faced ignominious ends. John had, it is true, lost Normandy, a fief which could

PREVIOUS PAGES The battle of Lincoln in 1217, when the supporters of the new King won a decisive victory over the rebellious barons. This and Hubert de Burgh's sea victory over Louis of France finally brought the civil war to an end.

204

The coronation of
Henry III, aged nine,
in 1216.

scarcely have been kept indefinitely by the rulers of England,
but at least he died fighting defiantly to preserve the unity of
his kingdom and the heritage of his son.

In fact John contributed notably to the relatively peaceful
succession of his son. In the first place, he had left behind him an
exceptionally able group of statesmen who were loyal to the
Angevin monarchy, including William Marshal who became
Protector or *rector* of the kingdom; Hubert de Burgh, the Chief

205

Justiciar, who gallantly defended the key town of Dover over many months; Ranulf of Chester, the most powerful baron in the north-west and Peter des Roches, the experienced and capable Bishop of Winchester. By his last campaign John had successfully cut off the King of the Scots and the unruly northerners from the barons who occupied London and the southern area of England which Louis of France had conquered. Thus the regency was left in good control of the west and the midlands. Henry III was crowned at Gloucester and the King's Council was able to meet in the port of Bristol, where it was decided to issue a revised version of John's Charter. Thus oaths were taken which constituted a first step towards reuniting the boy king with the English baronage. When in May 1217 the French and the dissident barons tried to break the hold of the royalists on central England they were utterly defeated in the battle of Lincoln. Afterwards Prince Louis was obliged to raise the siege of Dover and a French relieving force was destroyed at sea by the navy which John had created.

Several English kings have been dubbed the founders of the royal navy – Alfred the Great, Henry VIII, Charles I – but John has as good a claim as any. The early feudal method of raising a fleet was to commandeer ships and seamen from the barons of the Cinque ports – Hastings, Dover, Hythe, Romney and Sandwich – in the same way that the knights were called up from the service of their feudal superiors to form the royal armies, but in both cases these sailors and soldiers could only be required to fulfil the King's purposes for a limited period. John was extremely conscious of the importance of seapower and even of the value of economic sanctions maintained by naval blockade. It has been seen how John was thus able to exert pressure upon Flanders and to collect customs duties on trade with France, In 1216 John ordered English vessels not to trade with Scotland or other dominions belonging to his enemies. In his wars against both Wales and Ireland John made good use of his seapower. In order to do so John found it necessary to establish the nucleus of a royal navy. For that purpose he equipped galleys which were fitted with a sail and a mast but were normally moved by double banks of oarsmen. Either the enemy would be attacked with missiles – arrows fired by bowmen – or the galleys would be directed to ram the enemy's

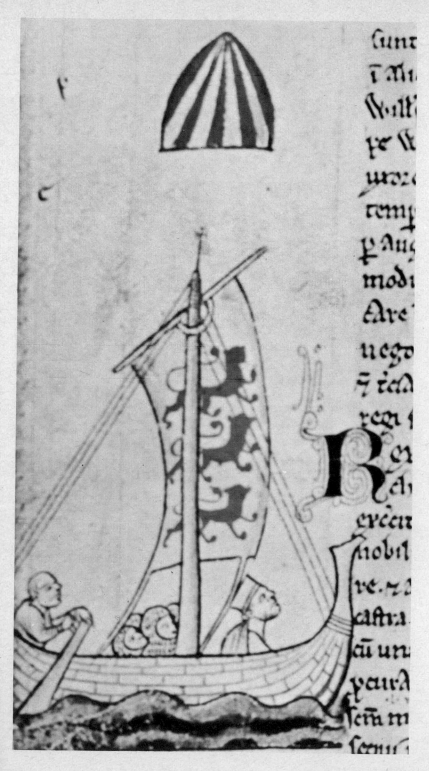

Henry III on his way to
Brittany to defend
his estates in France
in 1230.

A king with his bishops. In the Middle Ages kings approved and often nominated bishops so that they could count on their loyalty.

ships and then the men would board them. John, unlike his father or his brother, had a substantial number of galleys built for his own use as well as military transports. Galleymen were enlisted or impressed and paid at the relatively high rate of sixpence a day. But at the same time John insisted that all prize ships and goods captured from his enemies or from pirates were his to dispose of, though he sometimes gave the victorious galleymen half of the proceeds. The fruit of John's work in building up a royal navy was the great victory of Damme where three hundred French ships laden with corn, wine and arms were captured.

Historians have been divided over John's achievements as a military commander. He has, for example, been accused of 'lethargy' and 'mental disease' during the campaign that cost him the loss of Normandy and of having 'stayed in England biting his nails' when he should have been fighting upon the ramparts of Château-Gaillard. Yet the facts speak for themselves.

John showed himself to be a highly capable military organiser who was able to conjure up new armies whenever he needed them. The English barons, it is true, complained of the behaviour of the foreign mercenaries whom he recruited, claiming that they battened upon the English people. That was why the relatives of one of the mercenary captains, Gerard d'Athée, who had served John bravely and loyally as both seneschal of Touraine and castellan of Gloucester, were singled out in clause 50 of the Charter for removal from office and why clause 51 stipulated that as soon as peace had been restored the King was to expel from the country 'all foreign knights, crossbow-men, sergeants and mercenaries who had come with horse and arms to the detriment of the kingdom'.

Nevertheless John had done nothing new in recruiting such experienced officers and soldiers in preference to the untrained and disorderly feudal host. From the time of William the Conqueror all kings of England had made use of such mercenaries. They had fought at the battle of Hastings; they had served King Stephen; and they had proved indispensable to Henry II and Richard I as a permanent army for campaigns overseas. Henry II had also employed them in an emergency in England: that is what John did also, while, like his father, he relied on the feudal host for policing actions on the frontiers of Wales and Scotland. As to the character of the professional captains, whatever may have been said against Gerard d'Athée (who died before Runnymede), neither Savaric de Mauléon nor Falkes de Bréauté were unprincipled ruffians; they were strenuous and loyal commanders, nobles by birth, who served not only John but the regency of Henry III with conspicuous ability.

John's achievements as a general are obvious. He was not merely an excellent organiser and commander-in-chief, but a fighting general always ready to lead his men into the thick of battle. In his first war against Philip II he had been responsible for the victory at Mirebeau by heading a forced march of 80 miles in two days to surprise the enemy. His plan for the relief of Château-Gaillard in 1203 was worthy of his brother Richard, but it was an amphibious operation carried out by night and that is one of the most difficult actions in war. The reasons why John lost Normandy had nothing to do with lethargy or mental disease: the Norman barons turned against him and the English barons (such as Robert fitz Walter who pusillanimously handed over the castle at Vaudreuil without a fight) failed him. John then recognised that to regain Normandy required elaborate planning. He did not 'bite his nails' but awaited a more favourable opportunity after he had reorganised his forces and recruited his allies. The concepts of a pincer movement from both Normandy and Poitou in 1205 and from both Flanders and Poitou in 1214 were intelligent and realistic. But John's allies failed him, again not his mercenaries but his barons. Even his half-brother, William Longsword, the best of his native generals, was unable to win the battle of Bouvines or to occupy or retake London during the civil war. But John himself was almost invariably victorious, not only in Ireland and Wales but in Poitou and Gascony.

John was much more than a good soldier. He was also a

A scribe at work in a desk chair; his writing is supported by a book-rest.

hard-working and conscientious civil administrator. No king knew England – and especially the north of England – better than he did; and wherever he went, he brought justice and peace. He kept a close watch on the performance of his officials and changed his key men, the sheriffs, if he thought they had made themselves too unpopular or had fallen down on their jobs. He also tried to impose a check upon the profits made out of their offices by the sheriffs so that more money should flow into the Exchequer. As Dr Brian Harris has shown, he aimed to make the sheriffs into royal officials with an expense account, rather than tax farmers whose financial responsibilities ended after they had accounted for the shire farms. On the whole, this experiment was a success: sheriffs who failed to account satisfactorily for their profits were fined or dismissed.

John was extremely efficient at raising the money he required to pay for his wars. He needed to be because of the debts he had inherited from his predecessor and because of the pressure of inflation. Although it may be true that he did not possess as creative an administrative mind as his father, yet time was necessary to make Henry II's reforms work. It was here that John was effective in ensuring that the processes of the new justice were functioning. There was no real urgency for further reforms at that time. But John was creative in financial matters, for not only did he reorganise the monetary transactions of the sheriffs, but he introduced new taxes including customs duties and levies on property. He systematised some of the experiments undertaken by Richard I's officials to pay for his Crusade and ransom. It was the very thoroughness of John's financial measures which provoked the dissident barons into rebellion.

John's basic failure was of course that he proved unable to command the complete loyalty of his most powerful subjects. But that, after all, was a problem that confronted all English kings from the Normans to the Tudors. The interests of the monarch and the baronage were at root the same: they all wanted to uphold the same social system, for, if they could not work together, anarchy was liable to supervene. This problem has also coloured much later European history, but 'enlightened despots', once education became more widely spread, were able to draw upon a bureaucratic class to govern their countries and thus if they did not want to rely on their aristocracy they did not have to. John had no such choice. His chief servants were inevitably barons because there was no real alternative.

What John did, however, was to depend upon the ecclesiastical baronage for most of his leading officers of State, men like Hubert Walter, John de Gray and Peter des Roches. But his quarrel with the Church brought about the flight of nearly all the English bishops into exile abroad and that was a serious case of administrative weakness. It was here that John's judgment went astray. For however sound and hard-working a ruler he was himself, however able a general or clever a diplomatist, he had in the last resort to cope with individuals. To begin with, he mishandled his relations with Philip Augustus; then he had an unnecessary quarrel with William Marshal; he was initially unwise in his negotiations with Innocent III; and finally he alienated Stephen Langton after the Archbishop had been strikingly successful in acting as a mediator between John and his dissident barons. None of these disputes need have continued as long as they did, had John not been so stubborn or possibly over-clever. As Professor Holt has written, what he lacked was a level head.

John's reign was of significance because it included two events which were to prove signposts to the future: one was the sealing of the Charter at Runnymede, the other was the loss of Normandy by the King of England. It seems that it was John's original intention to abide by the clauses of the Charter, though he must have intensely disliked the idea of becoming the twenty-sixth petty king in the land. The news of the Charter's existence was made known and discussed throughout John's kingdom before it was annulled by the Pope. It 'was not merely circulated; it was proclaimed' (R.L.Poole). Although it is highly improbable that the sixty-three clauses were solemnly read out in Latin by the sheriffs in the shire courts, the fact that copies had been distributed to the remotest corners of the kingdom and that John gave orders not only to his sheriffs but to his foresters and bailiffs that the Charter should be publicly read, ensured that its terms became common knowledge everywhere. It was because of this wide circulation and because its contents had been discussed and debated by the representative gathering at Runnymede before John gave it his approval that the Charter has been called 'the first of English statutes'.

Though John died so soon after the enactment of the Charter that it is impossible to guess whether he might ultimately have put into practice some, though certainly not all, of its clauses, it is important to realise that John's most intimate friends and advisers, meeting at Bristol within a month after his death, confirmed the Charter of Liberties and that among those who confirmed it was the papal legate, Gualo, whose master had annulled it. These shrewd and experienced statesmen, meeting as Henry III's great Council of the realm, which was also the supreme court of justice in the kingdom, treated the Charter, shorn of its more doubtful clauses, including those relating to the watchdog committee of twenty-five barons, as if it were enacted law. In fact the Charter was to be confirmed many times in future Parliaments, was to be erected into 'the corner-stone of English liberties' and by the seventeenth century was conceived to have established the principles of no taxation without representation and no imprisonment of free men except by due process of law.

Indeed it may be argued that this was not such a gross distortion of what was actually determined during the reigns of John and his son as was once thought by those who considered the Charter to be the product of reactionary feudal barons. John promised by the Charter not to impose unreasonable scutages without the consent of his Great Council and not to prosecute or punish freemen except by the lawful judgment of their peers. Nor is it altogether fanciful to suggest that the great assembly at Runnymede foreshadowed the Parliaments called by John's son and grandson. In fact a clerk writing in 1244 spoke of 'the parliament at Runnymede'.

But even more significant for the future than the sealing and distribution of the Charter was the loss of Normandy. The Duke of Normandy had conquered England in 1066 and although he had promised to preserve the best of the Anglo-Saxon laws, the amalgamation of Normans and English did not advance very rapidly. With the accession of the Angevins things began to change, and Henry II's assizes reforming the criminal and civil law stamped England with a constitutional character of its own. Thus the reign of John, which ended exactly a hundred and fifty years after the Norman conquest, may be considered to be the culminating point in the growth

of a nation. Whereas William the Conqueror was described as the King of the Anglo-Normans, John was called King of England (*rex Angliae*) and no longer was there any discrimination between Normans and English. With the loss of Normandy, barons who held lands in the duchy as well as in England had to opt whether they would become Englishmen or Normans (William Marshal was the only notable exception). As has been seen, Gerald of Wales attributed the defeats suffered by King John and his allies to the determination of 'free Frenchmen': and he was far from wrong, for Philip Augustus has been hailed as one of the early fathers of French nationhood, who made Paris into a great capital and was the patron of the cathedral of Nôtre-Dame. Henceforward Normandy became a famous province of France, whereas England developed into a kingdom with a distinctive system of common law and justice and with an independent English ruling class. Within fifty years of John's death the beginnings of an English Parliament were to emerge.

Naturally John himself cannot be credited with deliberately forwarding the evolution of an independent nation. He did his utmost to reconquer Normandy and to preserve the Angevin inheritance. With his motley armies fighting in France against a rising tide of nationalism there, and dreaming sometimes of an international Crusade, he can hardly be fashioned into a hero of English nationhood. But this much may be said: John did think at times in terms of combining the different communities of the British Isles into one nation. The overlordship that he asserted in Scotland, the marriage of his daughter to a prince of Wales, his expedition to Ireland, all foreshadowed, however faintly, the United Kingdom of later times. Furthermore John, by his recognition of the value of seapower, his building of a navy and his victory over the French at sea – to be repeated during the regency which followed his death – showed some inkling of what was needed to convert England into a Great Power, as it was to be in the years to come. Possibly William Shakespeare was not so anachronistic as might be thought when he concluded his play *King John* with these lines:

> Come the three corners of the world in arms,
> And we shall shock them. Nought shall make us rue,
> If England to itself do rest but true.

215

Chronology

1167	24 December	John is born in Oxford.
1176	28 September	William, Earl of Gloucester, recognises John as his heir and John is betrothed to the Earl's youngest daughter, Isabella.
1185	24 April	John sails to Ireland.
1189	6 July	John's father, King Henry II, dies and he is succeeded by King Richard I, John's only surviving brother, who creates John Count of Mortain and assigns to him the revenues of six English counties.
1193	January	John concludes a treaty with King Philip II of France and tries to seize the throne during his brother's absence on Crusade, but is defeated by Richard I's Justiciars.
1194	May	Richard I, after release from imprisonment in Germany, forgives John for his treachery.
1199	6 April	Death of King Richard I.
	25 April	John is crowned Duke of Normandy.
	27 May	John is crowned King of England at Westminster.
1200	22 May	John concludes treaty of Le Goulet with King Philip II. Philip recognises John as King of England and John accepts Philip II as his overlord for Normandy and the Angevin possessions in France.
	26 August	After divorcing his first wife John marries Isabelle, daughter of Count Audemar of Angoulême.
1202	May	Philip II attacks Normandy and declares that John has forfeited his other fiefs in France which Philip bestows on John's nephew, Arthur of Brittany.
	1 August	John defeats Arthur of Brittany at Mirebeau in Anjou.
1203	3 April?	Arthur of Brittany executed in Rouen.
	5 December	John leaves Normandy.
1204	6 March	Surrender of Château-Gaillard in Normandy after seven months' siege.
	1 April	Death of John's mother, Eleanor of Aquitaine.
	24 June	Rouen, capital of Normandy, surrenders to French.
	October	John confiscates English lands of Norman barons who accept Philip as overlord.
1205	May	French forces overrun Poitou. John abandons expedition to Poitou on threat of invasion of England.
	6 December	John insists on the election of John de Gray, Bishop of Norwich, as successor to Hubert Walter as Archbishop of Canterbury.

1206	7 June	John lands at La Rochelle in Poitou and begins campaign in which he regains much of Aquitaine.
	26 October	Concludes truce with King Philip II for two years.
1207	17 June	Pope Innocent III consecrates Stephen Langton as Archbishop of Canterbury.
1208	23 March	Interdict imposed on England. John seizes property of clergy.
1209	7 August	After leading army to Scottish border John makes treaty with King William the Lion.
	November	John is excommunicated. Bishops withdraw from England.
1210	June–August	John asserts his authority in Ireland.
1211	July	After campaign in North Wales John concludes peace with Llewelyn the Great of Gwynedd.
1212	August	John abandons second campaign in Wales on learning of conspiracy by English barons to murder him.
1213	15 May	John ends quarrel with Pope Innocent III and swears fealty to him.
	30 May	John's half-brother, William, Earl of Salisbury, wins naval victory over French at Damme near Bruges.
	20 July	John welcomes Stephen Langton at Winchester where the Archbishop absolves him from excommunication.
	1 November	John interviews northern barons at Wallingford.
1214	2 February	John leaves England for campaign in France, landing at La Rochelle.
	13 June	Nantes surrenders to John.
	18 June	Angers surrenders to John.
	2 July	Interdict is lifted.
	9 July	John returns to La Rochelle after Poitevin barons refuse to fight against Prince Louis of France.
	27 July	John's allies defeated at battle of Bouvines.
	18 September	John concludes five-year truce with Philip II on the basis of *status quo*.
	15 October	John returns to England.
1215	6 January	John interviews barons in London.
	4 March	John takes oath as Crusader.
	12 May	Civil war begins.
	17 May	Dissident barons occupy London.
	29 May	John writes to Pope complaining about attitude of barons.
	15 June	Charter is sealed at Runnymede.
	19 June	John makes firm peace with dissident barons.
	16 July	John meets barons in Oxford.
	20 August	John refuses to meet barons again in Oxford.
	5 September	Papal commissioners denounce 'disturbers of realm' in accordance with papal mandate '*Mirari cogimur*' dated 7 June.
	September (end)	Papal bull '*Esti karissimus*' dated 24 August annulling Charter is published. Civil war is resumed.
	11 October	John captures Rochester.

1215	20 December	John decides on campaign in northern and eastern England.
1216	18 May	John's fleet is scattered by storm. Prince Louis of France, invited over by dissident barons, lands safely in England.
	5 June	John withdraws from Winchester into western England.
	3 September	John leaves western England to resume offensive against rebels in midlands.
	18 October	John dies at Newark and his embalmed body is sent for burial to Worcester Cathedral.

THE HOUSE OF PLANTAGENET

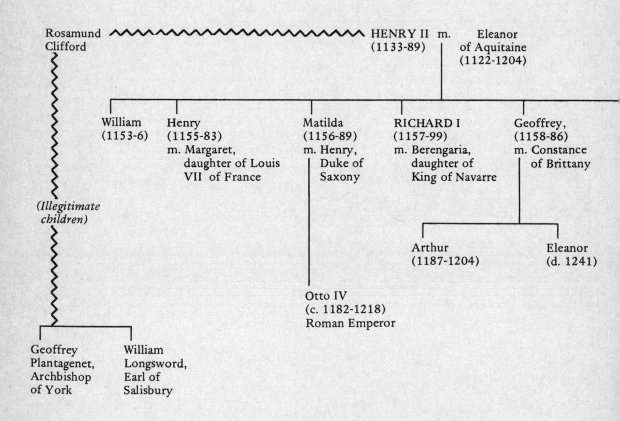

Rosamund Clifford ∿∿∿∿∿∿∿∿∿ HENRY II m. Eleanor
(1133-89) of Aquitaine
(1122-1204)

William
(1153-6)

Henry
(1155-83)
m. Margaret,
daughter of Louis
VII of France

Matilda
(1156-89)
m. Henry,
Duke of
Saxony

RICHARD I
(1157-99)
m. Berengaria,
daughter of
King of Navarre

Geoffrey,
(1158-86)
m. Constance
of Brittany

Arthur
(1187-1204)

Eleanor
(d. 1241)

Otto IV
(c. 1182-1218)
Roman Emperor

(Illegitimate
children)

Geoffrey
Plantagenet,
Archbishop
of York

William
Longsword,
Earl of
Salisbury

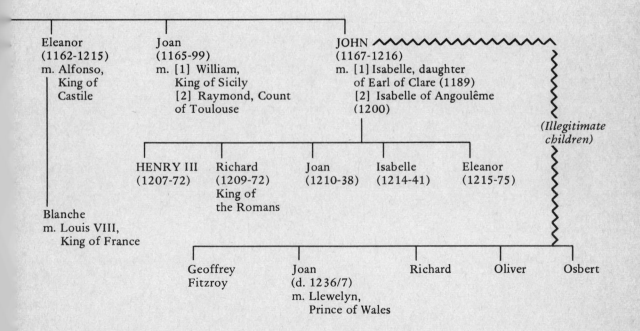

Eleanor
(1162-1215)
m. Alfonso,
    King of
    Castile

Joan
(1165-99)
m. [1] William,
    King of Sicily
    [2] Raymond, Count
    of Toulouse

JOHN
(1167-1216)
m. [1] Isabelle, daughter
    of Earl of Clare (1189)
    [2] Isabelle of Angoulême
    (1200)

(Illegitimate
children)

Blanche
m. Louis VIII,
    King of France

HENRY III
(1207-72)

Richard
(1209-72)
King of
the Romans

Joan
(1210-38)

Isabelle
(1214-41)

Eleanor
(1215-75)

Geoffrey
Fitzroy

Joan
(d. 1236/7)
m. Llewelyn,
    Prince of Wales

Richard

Oliver

Osbert

Select bibliography

The best introduction to the problems of the life of King John is the pamphlet written by J.C. Holt entitled *King John* (English Historical Association, 1970). An excellent exposure of some of the hoary chestnuts about John's life is to be found in H.G. Richardson and G.O. Sayles, *The Governance of Mediaeval England from the Conquest to Magna Carta* (1963) chap. XVII *seq*. The latest biography is that by W.L. Warren, *King John* (1961).

Below are listed a selection of books, pamphlets and articles about King John. They are mainly secondary authorities. No attempt has been made to list the chronicles and documents most of which are in Latin. Except where stated, all works were published in London.

BOOKS

John T. Appleby, *John King of England* (New York, 1959)

Frank Barlow, *The Medieval Kingdom of England 1042-1216* (1955; under revision)

R. Allen Brown, *English Castles* (1962)

H.E. Butler, *The Autobiography of Giraldus Cambrensis* (1937)

C.R. Cheney, *From Becket to Langton* (1955)
  Hubert Walter (1967)

C.R. Cheney and W.H. Semple, *Selected Letters of Innocent III concerning England 1198-1212* (1953)

W.L. Clowes, *The Royal Navy: a History*, vol. I (1897)

A. Duggan, *The Devil's Brood* (1957)

V.H. Galbraith, *Roger Wendover and Matthew Paris* (1944)

J.C. Holt, *The Northerners* (Oxford, 1962)
  Magna Carta (Cambridge, 1965)

A. Lane Poole, *Domesday Book to Magna Carta 1087-1216* (Oxford, 1951)

W.S. Mckechnie, *Magna Carta* (Glasgow, 1914)

Kate Norgate, *John Lackland* (1902)

Charles Oman, *A History of the Art of War in the Middle Ages*, vol. I (1924)

Sidney Painter, *William Marshal* (1933)
  The Reign of King John (Baltimore, 1949)

Charles Petit-Dutaillis, *Le Désheritement de Jean Sans Terre et le meurtre d'Arthur de Bretagne* (Paris, 1925)

F.M.Powicke, *Stephen Langton* (Oxford, 1928)

The Loss of Normandy (Manchester, 1963)

Doris M. Stenton, *English Society in the Early Middle Ages* (1971)

PAMPHLETS AND ARTICLES

Maurice Ashley, *Magna Carta in the Seventeenth Century* (Charlottesville, 1965)

C.R.Cheney, 'The Alleged Deposition of King John', *Studies presented to F.M.Powicke* (Oxford, 1948)

'The Eve of Magna Carta', *John Ryland's Library Bulletin* 38 (1956)

Brian Harris, 'King John and the Sheriffs' Farms', *English Historical Review*, July 1964

J.C.Holt, *The Making of Magna Carta* (Charlottesville, 1965)

E.F.Jacob, 'Innocent III', *Cambridge Medieval History*, vol. VI (1929)

Hilary Jenkinson, 'The Jewels lost in the Wash', *History*, October 1923

M.D.Knowles, 'The Canterbury Election of 1205–6', *English Historical Review*, 1938

R. Lane Poole, 'The Publication of Great Charters by English Kings', *English Historical Review*, 1913

Kate Norgate, 'The Alleged Condemnation of King John by the Court of France in 1202', *Transactions of the Royal Historical Society*, 1900

F.M.Powicke, 'Richard I and John', *Cambridge Medieval History*, vol. VI (1929)

H.G.Richardson, 'The Morrow of the Great Charter', *John Rylands Library Bulletin*, 1944 and 1945

'King John and Isabelle of Angoulême', *English Historical Review*, 1946 and 1950

Doris M. Stenton, 'King John and the Courts of Justice', *Proceedings of the British Academy*, 1958

After Runnymede: Magna Carta in the Middle Ages (Charlottesville, 1965)

A translation of Magna Carta is to be found in Professor Holt's book on the subject and also in Professor Warren's *King John*.

Index

uilipendentes. inestimabili gaudio perfusi
regis ⁊ filiu suu pedibus incuruati: sibi suoꝙ